EMPOWERED YOUTH

Mastering Emotions and Stress -
A CBT and DBT Guide for Teens

SKY BENSON

Empowered Youth

BY

(Sky Benson)

This is a work of creative nonfiction. Some parts have been fictionalized in varying degrees for various purposes.

Copyright © Sky Benson, 2024

Sky Benson

Email: info@skysplace.com

DISCLAIMER

The information provided in this guide is intended for informational and educational purposes only. It is not a substitute for professional advice, diagnosis, or treatment. Always seek the advice of qualified mental health professionals or other qualified health providers with any questions you may have regarding a medical or mental health condition. Never disregard professional medical advice or delay seeking it because of something you have read in this guide.

The authors and publishers of this guide are not responsible for any misuse of the information provided herein. Readers should use their discretion and consult with appropriate professionals for personalized guidance based on their circumstances.

Table of Contents

INTRODUCTION

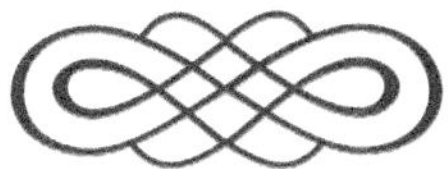

With the increasing number of issues related to mental health among young people, this resource, "Empowered Youth: Mastering Emotions and Stress - A CBT and DBT Guide for Teens," aims to provide guidance on how to cope. Building on the foundations of CBT and DBT, we will explore the complexities of this topic with the goal of equipping teenagers with healthy coping techniques.

Chapter by chapter, we delve into the world of adolescent mental health, covering topics including anxiety, depression, and other common problems. Adolescents can build the abilities necessary for emotional regulation and personal growth by learning about the basics of emotions and developing critical skills from dialectical behavior therapy (DBT) and cognitive behavioral therapy (CBT).

This manual serves as more than a theoretical reference; it is an actual tool for the job. We teach teens practical steps they can use every day, including advanced techniques for self-improvement, powerful activities, and journaling prompts. Combining CBT and

DBT, which are portrayed as a powerful team, offers a holistic strategy for mental health.

We hope that students, parents, and teachers will all discover helpful information and resources on this path to resilience. If we work together, we can create a world where young people's mental health is supported and encouraged.

CHAPTER 1

THE RISING TIDE OF YOUTH MENTAL HEALTH

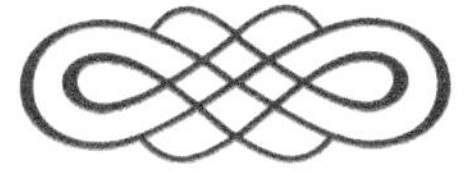

There is a mental health epidemic among children, and parents must do something about it.

In addition to killing hundreds of thousands of people, the epidemic has isolated us, severed ties to friends and family, and forced parents to stay home and raise their children in a single-income household. There have been enormous repercussions. One of these outcomes is the disturbing rise in adolescent and young adult sadness and anxiety.

Mental health is defined.

Have you ever experienced a sense of solitude? On occasion, do you experience feelings of self-hatred?

You will not be alone if you do this. Substance abuse and anger management are coping mechanisms for many young people who suffer from mental health concerns.

Mental health difficulties, like physical ones, can improve with time and treatment.

The term "mental health" is most often used to describe a person's emotional and psychological well-being.

When you're mentally well, you should be able to handle life and other people with ease and self-assurance. However, if your mental health isn't great, you may feel like you're not making it through life's challenges.

Having highs and lows is natural, and many people struggle with mental health concerns periodically. However, a mental disorder may be present if you sense that life is constantly becoming worse and that there is no way to improve your situation.

Treatment is necessary for those with mental diseases like depression, anxiety, and eating disorders because these conditions have a more significant influence on one's thoughts and actions than other mental health difficulties.

Teens' most prevalent mental health concerns

Feeling sad or angry is normal for people your age. Some prevalent thoughts include:

- Feeling alone,
- hating oneself,
- being bullied,
- being angry all the time,
- being in an abusive relationship,
- being overweight or underweight,
- wondering if one is gay or bisexual,
- drinking too much,
- having a drug problem,
- being a victim of sexual assault.

Suppose you suffer from suicidal thoughts or feelings. In that case, you are dealing with one of the most severe mental health disorders imaginable. Check out "Where to get help" down below if you're experiencing suicidal thoughts or self-harm.

Being a teenager is full of wonderful and challenging experiences, like learning to be independent, getting around high school, and making new friends. There are highs and lows to being a teenager in a world where the COVID-19 pandemic, social media, and distant learning are shaping our reality. The highs include things like acquiring our driver's license or passing that challenging exam.

The way teenagers take in information and use their time is very important since their brains are still learning and expanding. Every positive and negative event can affect their mental health.

Teens' mental health: a snapshot

A diagnosable mental health issue, like anxiety or depression, affects one out of five teenagers today. Worse yet, the prevalence of these mental problems among adolescents is becoming even higher. The prevalence of mental problems among adolescents is, according to specialists, at an all-time high.

Trauma, Borderline Personality Disorder, schizophrenia, and depression are among the mental health concerns that can affect teenagers. In addition, adolescent mental health issues include behavioral disorders such as substance misuse and food disorders.

Symptoms of mental illness in teenagers can be hard to spot. The reason is that adolescence is a time of tremendous emotional and physical upheaval for the majority of teens. On the other hand, adolescent mental illness is characterized by far more severe than usual shifts in mood and behavior.

There are many emotional highs and lows in a young person's life, despite the common belief that they are less severe than adults. Statistics on adolescent and teen mental health make this point extremely clear; up to 20% of this age group exhibit symptoms of a diagnosable mental disease. At the time a person reaches the ages of 14 and 24, half of all cases of mental illness will have manifested at that point in their lives.

Severe Adolescent Depression

Depression is among the most prevalent mental health issues affecting American youth and young adults. A new survey shows that the number of people diagnosed with severe depression has increased by 33% since 2013. Statistical data on adolescent mental health also indicates that this rate is 47% higher among millennials. In addition, there has been a 47% increase in the rates of major depression in males and a 65% increase in the rates for girls among adolescents.

The negative mood that lasts for two weeks or longer and is evident in most situations is the hallmark of a major depressive episode. A lack of confidence, disinterest in formerly pleasurable hobbies, and difficulties with sleep, energy, and focus are all signs. Everyday tasks like working, studying, sleeping, and eating become incredibly challenging, if not impossible, for teens suffering from severe depression. In addition, the likelihood of experiencing a second episode of major depressive illness is considerable for people who have already experienced one.

There are a few other names for major depression, including clinical depression and major depressive disorder. It features some of the most debilitating symptoms of any depression kind.

So, it can come on suddenly and linger for a while. Teens' quality of life is, therefore, profoundly impacted.

Anxiety in Teens

It's not always easy to recognize when normal adolescent tension becomes anxious. But, heightened anxiety is a hallmark of adolescent anxiety disorders. On top of that, instead of getting better on their own, these emotions only worsen with time.

In addition, the stress and worry that adolescent sufferers of anxiety disorders experience on a daily basis can get in the way of their success in the classroom and on the job. Adolescent anxiety, like other adolescent mental disorders, impacts how teenagers interact with their loved ones and classmates.

When it comes to anxiety disorders among teenagers, GAD is by far the most common. Anxiety disorders in teenagers include an unhealthy preoccupation with mundane matters. In addition, the anxiousness persists for a very long time. In addition to a wide array of anxiety-related symptoms, teenagers who suffer from generalized anxiety disorder endure significant emotional distress. In addition, youth who suffer from GAD often struggle with low self-esteem and excessive worrying.

Adolescent Eating Disorders

Eating disorders in adolescents encompass binge eating disorder, bulimia, and anorexia. Death rates from anorexia nervosa, whether from starvation, metabolic collapse, or suicide, are the greatest of any psychiatric condition. As a result, it ranks high among the most hazardous mental diseases affecting teenagers.

Teens' physical health and eating habits are severely disrupted by adolescent eating disorders. Teens' emotional well-being is also impacted. There is nearly always another mental health issue present alongside an eating disorder.

Moodiness, anxiety, and depression are common symptoms among adolescents who suffer from teen eating disorders. Teens who struggle with anorexia are more likely to engage in risky behaviors such as substance addiction and self-harm.

Addiction to Substances

Substance use disorder is known as a psychiatric condition in adolescents. For many young people, substance abuse is a means of coping with emotional and mental health issues such as sadness, anxiety, trauma, and low self-esteem.

A poor and even harmful coping method for symptoms of adolescent mental problems is substance usage. And addiction can develop with continued use. According to research, the following things make someone more likely to have a substance use disorder:

- An inherited tendency
- The Green movement's endorsement of extensive drug usage
- Peer pressure is a factor.

Anxiety Disorders in Adolescents

A secure sense of identity is absent in adolescents who have borderline personality disorder. Because of this, adolescents who have borderline personality disorder are emotionally illiterate. People who have borderline personality disorder are highly emotionally unstable because they lack a stable sense of self.

Additionally, young people and teenagers are common onset years for borderline personality disorder. Teens who have borderline personality disorder often struggle to form meaningful relationships. As a result, people end up feeling hopeless and alone. They experience disarray and anxiety due to a lack of self-awareness. Consequently, situations and encounters that ought to be manageable become challenging.

Adolescent Psychosis

Chronic schizophrenia is a disorder that persists throughout a person's life. Another aspect is that adolescence is when the symptoms of schizophrenia first show. The National Institute of Mental Health reports that symptoms of schizophrenia typically manifest in individuals under the age of 30. Schizophrenic adolescents struggle to understand and manage their feelings. A lot of the time, they even separate themselves from reality.

Brain anatomy, chemistry, and processing abilities are all different in people who have schizophrenia. As a result, learning new things and comprehending complex knowledge is challenging for people with schizophrenia. This makes it more challenging for individuals to manage their illness fully. Thus, educating the patient and encouraging them to manage their condition actively is the primary objective of schizophrenia treatment.

Teen Trauma and PTSD

Direct or indirect victims of catastrophic events may continue to feel the repercussions of the tragedy long after it has passed. Chronic stress disorder (PTSD) is a possible outcome of such traumatic experiences. Adverse events, such as fires, crimes, childhood maltreatment, the death of a parent or other family member, and other catastrophic events, can lead to post-traumatic stress disorder (PTSD) in adolescents.

Acute trauma refers to a single traumatic occurrence. Mental health issues, including traumatic stress disorder (PTSD) and acute trauma, can manifest in adolescents. After a traumatic event has occurred, the effects of the stress may not go away for a long time.

"Chronic trauma" refers to traumatic experiences that continue over time, such as seeing or experiencing domestic violence, gang violence, or maltreatment in childhood. Acute and chronic trauma are both potential causes of post-traumatic stress disorder in adolescents.

Substance Use Disorders in Adolescents

In addition to the more typical mental health issues, teenagers might suffer from less prevalent mental health diseases as well. Some examples of these are:

Attention Deficit Hyperactivity Disorder

Because of its impact on learning and behavior, Attention Deficit Hyperactivity Disorder (ADHD) is usually detected early on in adolescents, despite the disorder's prevalence. Estimates put the prevalence of ADHD in children and adolescents with a range of 4–17 years old at around 9%. These kids could be energetic and impulsive, have trouble focusing, and have trouble ignoring distractions.

Some of the symptoms of attention deficit hyperactivity disorder (ADHD) in children and teenagers include:

- hopping from one activity to another without warning,
- easily becoming bored with a task,
- having trouble concentrating or paying attention,
- having trouble finishing schoolwork,
- having difficulty processing information quickly,
- having trouble sitting still,
- touching or playing with everything,
- acting carelessly,
- talking excessively,
- interrupting others.

A child's capacity to learn is impacted by ADHD, which frequently necessitates a creative approach both at home and in school. Thus, it may be crucial for your adolescent's future achievement to identify and address this condition. The fact that about two-thirds of children diagnosed with ADHD also deal with another condition is crucial information for parents to have. Conditions such as anxiety, depression, or a learning handicap may fall under this category. It is advised that individuals who suffer from numerous or co-occurring mental health illnesses undergo integrated dual-diagnosis treatment.

Narcissistic Personality Disorder:

While it disproportionately affects the young, it affects about 6% of the population nationally. An example of a narcissistic trait is an exaggerated sense of self-importance and accomplishment. Narcissists also have trouble putting themselves in another person's shoes.

Obsessive-Compulsive Disorder:

The anxiety disorder known as Obsessive-Compulsive Disorder (OCD) can strike at any age, from toddlers and teenagers to adults.

Histrionic Personality Disorder:

Adolescents with Histrionic Personality Disorder have a tendency to exaggerate their emotions and the gravity of their circumstances.

Dissociative Identity Disorder:

Dual or multiple personality states are symptoms of Dissociative Identity Disorder (DID), a medical diagnosis. Trauma or abuse is a common experience for those with dissociative identity disorder.

Gaming Disorder:

A mental health issue the World Health Organization has just lately labeled gaming disorder. Those who suffer from gaming problems are not unlike those who struggle with substance misuse or gambling addiction. To sum up, compulsive video game playing is a hallmark of this disease.

What Leads to Mental Health Issues in Adolescents

The causes of the alarming rise in adolescent mental problems are a topic of much debate among experts. Most importantly, they think that multiple of these factors may have an impact on teenagers.

- First, research has linked adolescent screen time with mental health issues. The time and effort put into relationships, schoolwork, and extracurricular activities is drained when one spends too much time in front of a screen. The researchers concluded that the increases in depression and suicide among iGen adolescents might be attributed to their increased time spent on new media screen activities and decreased time spent on non-screen activities since 2010.

- Also, a lot of the stress and worry that teenagers feel comes from social media. Unfavorable comparisons with the lives of the individuals they follow on social media platforms like Instagram, Twitter, and Facebook can lead to depression among teenagers.

- Many teenagers also feel academic pressure. This stress is intensified by an unstable economy and fierce competition for undergraduate, graduate, and professional programs.

♦ In addition, the coping abilities of today's youth are lacking. Their parents do their best to protect their children from the pain of setbacks and disappointments. Teens are thus less likely to have opportunities to develop resilience. Because of this, they never master the art of dealing with adversity.

♦ The brain continues to develop throughout adolescence. Therefore, the area of the brain responsible for self-regulation, the prefrontal cortex, has yet to develop in adolescents fully. Because of this, people aren't very good at controlling their impulses. Adolescents engage in risky activities like substance misuse and make unsafe sexual decisions as a result.

♦ Adolescents don't get enough fresh air and exercise because they are glued to their devices. Therefore, they are suffering from NDD, a term first used by Richard Louv in Last Child in the Woods (2005). A variety of behavioral and mental health issues manifest in children and teenagers as a result of their reduced outside time.

Why are adolescent mental health issues on the rise?

Adolescent mental illness is not necessarily a recent phenomenon. Some commonalities often herald the start of mental health problems, the majority of which manifest throughout adolescence. For instance, both physically and socially, adolescents are undergoing profound changes. They are under more pressure than ever to find their place among their classmates and prove themselves. Problems with self-esteem, substance abuse, behavioral disorders, and stress levels all rise in tandem with this. Symptoms of mental health issues may manifest as a result of this.

But why are mental health issues among teenagers becoming more common? For what reasons are these numbers going up?

The increase in adolescent mental health disorders prior to the pandemic should be our primary focus. These numbers can be explained in several ways, including:

- Talking about mental health is growing in frequency and openness. When compared to previous generations, today's youth are far more open and forthcoming about talking about their struggles with mental health. This has led to an increase in the number of people seeking assistance and sharing personal stories of hardship.

- Young people's lives are now heavily reliant on social media. Adolescents always see pictures of people with flawless looks or ideal lives. Youth's mental health suffers as a result of the pressure they feel to conform to unrealistic standards of beauty and behavior on social media. • Academic pressure is on the rise among youth. More and more young people are under pressure to excel academically and professionally due to rising levels of competition in both the classroom and the workplace. More stress and substance abuse may result from this than what is indicated by past trends.

- Adolescents often deal with substance misuse. Nearly two-thirds of high school kids have consumed alcohol, and approximately half have used marijuana by the time they reach the 12th grade, according to estimates. Adolescent mental health issues are associated with substance misuse. Substance abuse is hurting young people's mental health as its rates continue to rise.

♦ Our young people are worried about macro-level stresses. Nowadays, Young people care more than simply making friends and doing well in school. Beyond that, they care about the bigger picture in their communities. Unfortunately, today, we must contend with climate change, financial problems, gun violence, inequality, and racism. Many young people are actively working to change the world they will inherit. This, in turn, adds more pressure on teens, who may already be struggling with mental health issues, including despair, anxiety, and hopelessness.

All of the things above are just a few of the many causes of the present mental health epidemic. The COVID-19 pandemic's effects are also impossible to overlook.

While the epidemic had a profound impact on all of us, it was especially hard on American youth. Adolescents were cut off from their classmates and peers at a time when they needed each other the most. Staying home, attending lectures electronically, and missing out on milestone social occasions were all consequences of their forced isolation. They had to deal with the pandemic's economic toll, worries about the virus, the loss of loved ones, and diminished access to healthcare, all while. "School closures, social isolation, family economic hardship, fear of family loss or illness, and reduced access to health care because of inadequate insurance coverage or medical office closures and reduced hours" were some of the ways the pandemic impacted the mental health of young people, according to the CDC.

The CDC released additional data about adolescent struggles:

- 5% of pupils reported that they were victims of emotional abuse at home during the pandemic.

- During the same period, 11% were victims of physical abuse at home.

- Nearly one-third of high school students said that someone in their immediate family had lost their job.

- During the pandemic, 24% of teenagers reported feeling hungry.

- Since the pandemic started, two-thirds of the students reported having trouble with their homework.

In addition to these difficulties, the proliferation of COVID-19 brought about loss and disease. During the COVID-19 pandemic, the virus affected millions of people, and according to contemporary statistics, over 140,000 children in the United States lost a primary or secondary caregiver. Minority youth have suffered an outsized share of the effects.

We are caring for youths whose skyrocketing rates of sadness, anxiety, trauma, loneliness, and suicidality will have long-lasting effects on them, their families, communities, and our collective futures, according to the American Academy of Pediatrics. Doing nothing will not work. We must act quickly and systematically because this is a national emergency.

When we're in a mood, it's not always about feeling lonely, angry, or disappointed.

Difficulties with mental health are distinct from temporary low mood or exhaustion. They're more substantial, they linger for longer, and they disrupt regular life in significant ways. A few examples of common mental health issues include trauma, anxiety, depression, eating disorders, and substance abuse. They can disrupt a teen's regular routine and influence their thoughts, feelings, and actions.

Worrying even more: Adolescents often struggle with mental health issues. The majority of mental health issues (up to 75%) tend to manifest throughout adolescence. The Mental Health First Aid (MHFA) program reports that one out of five teenagers will have a severe mental health illness during their lifetime.

Although not all mental health issues will be officially recognized as mental disorders, it is important to treat every difficulty with the seriousness it deserves.

Consider the ways in which substance abuse, changes in food habits and sleep patterns, and other behavioral changes can have an effect on one's physical health when left untreated. An emerging mental health issue, such as depression or substance abuse illness, may be indicated by symptoms of exhaustion, social withdrawal, or changes in mood.

Spending more time with friends, developing a distinct sense of self, and learning to fend for themselves are all hallmarks of adolescence. A mental health issue can interfere with or even obstruct all of these experiences, which are vital to their growth.

The consequences of ignoring a mental health issue, depending on its severity, might linger far into adulthood.

What steps can be taken to safeguard the mental health of adolescents?

Teens require resources to help them communicate their feelings and respond to friends' attempts to connect with them. The likelihood of an adolescent confiding in a friend rather than an adult is higher, according to the research.

That's why it's crucial to have open conversations with teenagers about the difficulties they can face when they enter adulthood. Feelings of sadness, anger, isolation, and frustration are normal, and they need to know that. Teens need to be able to detect the early warning signals so they can seek the care they need when they need it. Still, chronic difficulties could be an indication of something else entirely. Young adult Emotional Well-Being Students in tenth through twelfth grades learn the basics of mental health first aid, including how to recognize the symptoms of a friend experiencing a crisis and how to respond appropriately, as well as when to seek help from an adult they trust. The good news is that there is hope for many troubled kids who seek help for their mental health or drug use issues. Seeking assistance is the initial stage.

The significance of efficient coping strategies in the age of technology

There is a constant and overwhelming amount of change. That remains true regardless of the nature of the change—whether it's anticipated or not.

Finding a technique to deal with new stresses while maintaining emotional stability is a constant goal whenever anything unexpected arises in life. Emotions are difficult to navigate and manage without coping techniques, which you may or may not be conscious of.

To be more precise, how do coping mechanisms work?

Tell me about ways to deal with stress.

A person's coping strategies are the routines and practices they employ when faced with extreme stress. Until they can completely adapt to the change, humans rely on these tactics to keep themselves calm.

Picture yourself boarding a boat. Stepping onto the deck causes the boat to begin to sway under your feet. Until you get your balance, you cling tenaciously to the railing. Just a little while after that, you and a friend are standing on the boat having a conversation when it starts to move. You falter, seeking a helping hand.

The changes in your situation are like the waves on the water. Your natural inclination to seek assistance is a way for you to cope. Like any good sailor will tell you, some aspects of life are easier to cling to than others. Find out what makes you feel secure, and hold on to those things when times go tough.

Three ways to deal with stress

Coping methods aren't a magic bullet. Situations or circumstances outside of their control, known as stressors, are the usual culprits. There are two main ways that people deal with stressful situations: problem-focused coping and emotion-focused coping.

Taking action to obtain assistance or find a solution that makes the situation easier to handle is an example of problem-focused coping. The goal of emotion-focused coping is to alleviate the emotional discomfort that accompanies a stressful situation.

There is no inherent superiority between the two coping mechanisms. Sometimes, like after a loved one's death, there's nothing you can do to alter the course of events. When it happens, all you can do is control how you react. However, you likely employ a combination of the two kinds when confronted with challenging situations.

I'll give you an example: Upon reviewing your credit card statement, you see several charges that are unexpected to you. You justify your growing unease by telling yourself that the objects must indeed belong to a relative. After consulting with everyone, it is now obvious that the charges are false. Possible ways of coping include:

1. Dealing with problems

You notify the bank immediately by calling them and explaining the situation. You put a freeze on the accounts and your credit record to prevent any additional harm. The next step is to prepare for future expenses by making a list of everything you need to buy.

2. Dealing with Emotions

After taking a brief moment to sit quietly, you go for your phone and place an order for your go-to takeout—just what you need to boost your mood. Finally, you break it to your significant other and air your grievances; after that, you put in a movie to take your mind off of things.

3. A mixed-method reaction

You decide to contact a friend who has recently been in a similar predicament. They understand how aggravating it is, and they want you to know that it happens sometimes. In addition to advising you to contact your bank immediately, your friend walks you through the process step by step. Once you've contacted the bank, you settle down to watch a show that brings you comfort. You will return to canceling and replacing the remaining cards once you feel somewhat better.

As active coping mechanisms, problem-focused and emotion-focused approaches are equally valid. These are some preventative measures you can take to lessen or eliminate stress. In contrast to reactive coping mechanisms, which are often harmful or counterproductive, adaptive coping mechanisms teach you how to change with the times.

Adaptation strategies vs. protection mechanisms

Protective mechanisms are a subset of coping strategies. They usually only manifest when you're feeling stressed within. In response to stressful, upsetting, or otherwise identity-threatening stimuli, the unconscious mind employs a variety of defense strategies.

When you're employing a coping mechanism to manage stress, you usually become aware of it. However, you may be unaware of your actions when utilizing protection mechanisms. Maybe the circumstance is so terrifying that you can't bring yourself to do anything about it, not even acknowledge, deny, or suppress it. This is unhealthy because it doesn't deal with the source of the stress or the problem at hand, unlike active coping mechanisms.

How crucial coping strategies are to overall health

Is the saying "Control only what you can control" something you're familiar with? Dealing with stress is clearly addressed. When things get out of hand, your coping mechanisms kick in and help you get back on track. Either attempting to manage your emotions or finding a solution to the problem will accomplish the trick.

When you're feeling overwhelmed by stress and frustration, a healthy coping method might help you regain your equilibrium. You enter "problem-solving" mode subconsciously when you employ coping mechanisms. When you talk about how you deal with things, you usually bring up the aspects of a scenario over which you do have some say, such as how you react to it.

The term "internal locus of control" describes how you feel about your own agency in making a positive change in your life. A strong sense of internal locus is associated with better physical health, higher levels of happiness, and six times the likelihood of resilience.

Those whose control is situated outside of themselves are less likely to take the initiative to achieve their goals because they depend on other people or factors to guide their actions and decisions. A lack of control over some aspects of your life isn't necessarily a bad thing. Still, it might cause you to feel hopeless and resort to harmful coping techniques.

Taking responsibility for what we can influence, even if it's only our emotional response to our situation, can have a significant impact on our outcomes. As a result of our improved mood, the situation often appears more favorable. This lessens the chances of experiencing mental health issues like sadness, anxiety, low self-esteem, and unhealthy ways of dealing with stress.

You can make a huge difference in the results when you control what you can, even if it's only your emotional response to situations. No matter what happens, when you feel better about the situation, it always seems better.

Taking a step back is a great place to start when you're feeling overwhelmed by life's happenings. We can reframe the circumstance and get some perspective if we do this. Problems are easier to overcome when we approach them with a positive outlook. Optimal coping mechanisms center on maintaining a positive emotional state as you face the challenge.

When we are overwhelmed and unable to take any positive action, unhealthy coping mechanisms typically come into play. If you want to overcome obstacles and keep moving forward, make a note of what sets you off and discuss them with a coach.

CBT and DBT, the two main forms of behavior modification

For many psychiatric diseases, psychotherapy is among the most effective treatment options. Among the many therapeutic approaches available, Cognitive Behavioral Therapy (CBT) stands out. Communicating your issues aloud might help you reframe them, which is the main goal of cognitive behavioral therapy (CBT), sometimes known as talk therapy.

"I am a failure" could be a controlling negative thought pattern. There is nothing I can do correctly. When people see me for who I truly am, they will hate me. - Cognitive behavioral therapy (CBT) can teach you to stop letting your ideas rule you and start doing the opposite by applying logic and reason.

The core tenet of cognitive behavioral therapy (CBT) is the belief that we can improve our emotional well-being by altering our mental and behavioral responses to challenging events.

However, not all mental diseases respond well to conventional CBT. A second popular kind of treatment is DBT or Dialectical Behavior Therapy. Differentiated behavior therapy (DBT) is a subset of cognitive behavioral therapy (CBT) that aims to teach people who have trouble controlling their emotions to engage with the world around them more rationally and healthily.

Is there much of a difference between CBT and DBT since their names are so similar? Is there a benefit to using one over the other? Keep reading to find out what sets you apart.

Chapter 2

Understanding Emotions: The First Step to Regulation

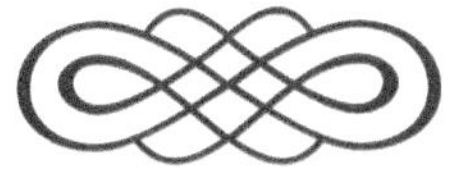

Feelings are essential to living each day. They also fluctuate in the here and now. Teens may find it difficult to regulate their emotions due to hormonal changes, chronic stress, and an absence of mental health resources. Because of this, a lot of young people may start abusing substances.

Substance abuse may offer a short reprieve from painful emotions. Still, as the effects of the substance wear off, the emotions will resurface. Helping adolescents learn to recognize and manage their emotions is one of the primary goals of mental health treatment programs.

What Emotions Can Teach Us

As you begin to read this, how are you currently feeling? Is curiosity piqued? Are you hoping to gain some self-discovery? Feeling bored because you have to do this for school even though you're not enthusiastic about it, or joyful because it's an enjoyable school project? Maybe you're too preoccupied with other feelings, like anticipation of the weekend or grief over a recent split, to pay attention to the task at hand.

These kinds of feelings are normal for humans. In doing so, they inform us about our experiences and guide our responses.

Even as infants, we are able to detect and label our feelings. Facial expressions and gestures such as laughing, snuggling, and weeping are ways in which infants and young children show their emotions. They exhibit emotional behavior but lack the language skills to describe their feelings or articulate the reasoning behind them.

Understanding and managing our emotions is a talent that develops throughout life. We may stop responding impulsively and start expressing ourselves instead of acting like children. We become more adept at identifying our emotions and their causes as we gain experience and maturity. This ability is known as emotional intelligence.

When we are in tune with our emotions, we can identify our wants, needs, and needs (or lack thereof). Our relationships are strengthened as a result. The reason behind this is that being in tune with our emotions allows us to express ourselves more accurately, handle disputes more effectively, and overcome challenging emotions with ease.

The ability to feel and express one's emotions comes more easily to certain people than to others. Fortunately, being more self-aware of one's emotions is something that anyone can do. Practice is all it takes. However, the work is worthwhile: A person's ability to thrive in life depends on their level of emotional intelligence, which can be developed through practicing emotional awareness.

Emotions 101

To begin, here are some fundamentals regarding emotions:

- ◆ Feelings are transitory. The majority of us experience a wide range of emotions on a daily basis. Some of them don't even last a minute. A mood may emerge from some of the others.

♦ On the spectrum from moderate to intense, or anywhere in between, are emotions. Both the circumstance and the individual can influence the degree to which an emotion is felt.

♦ Although feelings are neutral, there are appropriate and inappropriate methods to show or act upon them. The ability to understand emotions is the cornerstone of the other skill known as "emotion management," which is learning appropriate ways to express one's feelings.

Everything is OK

When we experience positive emotions, including joy, love, confidence, inspiration, enthusiasm, interest, thankfulness, or inclusion, it might make us feel good. Some feelings, like anger, resentment, fear, humiliation, guilt, sadness, or worry, can appear more negative. Feelings of joy and sorrow are equally natural.

We can learn something about ourselves and our circumstances from every feeling. However, there are moments when we struggle to acknowledge our emotions. When we experience negative emotions, like jealousy, for instance, we may be too hard on ourselves. However, we should pay more attention to our feelings rather than trying to convince ourselves that we shouldn't.

Negative emotions might backfire if we try to suppress them or act as though they don't exist. When we avoid confronting and making sense of our negative emotions, we make it more difficult to let them go and fade. No need to wallow in self-pity or bring up your feelings all the time. Said emotional awareness is the ability to notice, label, and cope with one's emotional experiences as they unfold.

Raising Self-Awareness

Developing self-awareness and acceptance requires emotional intelligence. How can you train yourself to pay more attention to your feelings? Here are three easy steps to get started:

1. Develop the practice of regularly checking in with your emotions in various contexts throughout the day. Making preparations to travel somewhere with a friend may cause you to feel a surge of excitement. Or perhaps you have anxiety just before a test. Music may put you at peace, art can move you, and receiving praise from a buddy can make your day. All you have to do is pay attention to your feelings and mentally label them. Doing this will help you a lot, and it won't even take a second. Take note that you might move on to other feelings as you go through life.

2. Please indicate the intensity of your emotion. The next stage, after recognizing and labeling an emotion, is to: On a scale from 1 (very mild) to 10 (very intense), please indicate the degree to which you experience this emotion.

3. Let those closest to you in on how you're feeling. This is the most effective method for honing the art of expressive writing, which brings us closer to everyone we know: parents, coaches, friends, and romantic partners. Communicate your emotions to someone you trust at least once a day. Something incredibly intimate or just an ordinary feeling could be shared.

Feelings Explained

Thoughts, deeds, feelings, and memories all contribute to the development of emotional states. Laughter, sobs, a constriction of the chest, and other bodily sensations are all manifestations of emotions, which have their roots in the brain. Regrettably, in modern culture, people hardly ever talk about their feelings.

The following are examples of common emotions:

- Joy
- Sadness
- Grief
- Anger
- Happiness
- Ecstasy
- Shame
- Guilt
- Fear
- Anxiety

Instead of teaching teens about emotions and how they impact our lives, we often tell them to keep their feelings under check. The ability to identify, label, and work with one's emotions is a challenge for many.

Skills for Emotional Regulation: What Are They?

Competences in controlling one's emotions are exactly what they sound like. They are acquiring the skill of controlling their emotions. Feelings, ideas, and reactions are the building blocks of emotions, making them malleable. Emotions, in fact, vary throughout the day. After experiencing sadness, you could feel guilty or amused. Our upbringing, our beliefs, and our emotional intelligence all play a role in shaping our emotional responses to our ideas and the environment.

Emotion regulation is difficult for many people. Outbursts of violent behavior, self-harm, isolating oneself, and substance use are common outcomes of this. There is no longer any need for drugs, alcohol, or other destructive behaviors when individuals engage with therapists to improve their capacity to endure painful feelings, control emotional states, and change emotions.

Emotional Intelligence

Having a good grasp of one's own emotions and the ability to articulate and convey them clearly can contribute to improved mental health and recovery from mental illness.

Recognizing Feelings

Although it may be difficult to put oneself in the shoes of an unfamiliar emotion, this section offers advice on recognizing and accepting one's sentiments.

Robert Plutchick developed the emotions wheel, sometimes known as the "Plutchick Wheel," in 2001. Its purpose is to help people become more emotionally literate by teaching them to recognize and describe a variety of feelings. It is possible to better recognize one's own emotions if one is familiar with the variety of human feelings and the distinctions between them.

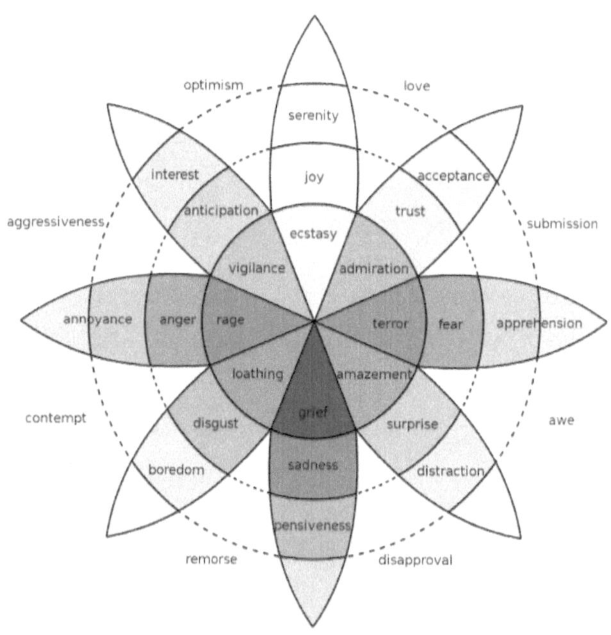

The first step in understanding and managing an emotion is to recognize and name it; this is achieved by moving outward from the center of the wheel, which represents the emotional experience.

Conveying Feelings

Using a traffic light system and attentive action matching, this part explains how to better utilize emotions. By accepting and acting on one's true emotions, one might learn to live a more genuine life.

Even though it may seem childish at first, traffic lights can really assist adults and teenagers in articulating their feelings in a more controllable way.

Carrying a miniature traffic light picture in one's pocket or bag allows one to swiftly evaluate one's emotional state; green denotes contentment, happiness, and positivity; amber, uncertainty, on edge, and concern; and red, agitation, upset, anger, and illness. The traffic lights can be a useful tool for keeping track of one's emotions in public or for communicating with loved ones or caregivers.

Here are a few examples:

While you're out shopping, your heart races at the sight of all the people. You whip out your traffic signals and notice that the green light has become orange. You opt to use the self-checkout so you may avoid approaching strangers. As soon as you exit the store, you begin formulating a strategy to go from amber to green.

After a fight with your parents, you retreat to your bedroom, where you can see your emotions flashing red. When you give yourself time to relax (by doing things like listening to music, chatting with friends online, or taking a lengthy shower), you might feel like you've reached a turning point. You should now go downstairs and inform your folks that you're feeling much better. Attempt to resolve the issue in a more composed manner.

Keep in mind that everyone's traffic light system is different; it might be useful to make a list of feelings that correspond to each color. One can learn to express their emotions appropriately by engaging in activities that match the emotion they are experiencing after using the emotions wheel and the traffic light system. The greatest method to be kind to oneself is to match emotions deliberately with actions; this will aid in the maintenance and regulation of mental well-being.

Some examples include:

- Take a break from a particularly difficult assignment and replace it with something more relaxing, like self-care, until the anger subsides.

- You can avoid the anxiety and stress that comes with going grocery shopping in a crowded store by ordering online and having them delivered.

- When you're experiencing strong emotions like excitement, hyperactivity, or emptiness, it's better to engage in a creative hobby than to spend money impulsively.

Coping with challenging feelings

In this part, we'll examine some of the methods for gaining insight into and mastery over unpleasant emotions like wrath, despair, fear, etc. A lot of people don't know what to do when they have these feelings, which may be quite upsetting.

Unfortunately, bad feelings are universal and never go away. Even if it's scary to feel strong negative emotions like anger, you should know that these feelings are temporary and not hazardous. Emotions come and go.

No matter how bad or nice someone may be, the fact that they feel horrible about themselves does not make them a bad person. When handled constructively, negative emotions like hate, annoyance, resentment, etc., towards another person are entirely normal.

Healthy psychological development and the avoidance of suppressed emotional overwhelm are both promoted by being kind to oneself and by allowing unpleasant feelings to be voiced when necessary.

Resolving difficult feelings in a healthy and controlled manner can be a liberating experience. Converting unpleasant thoughts and feelings into something more manageable requires learning to channel negative emotions into productive expression. When we create art from our deepest, darkest emotions, we have the power to transform our sorrow into a sense of accomplishment, fulfillment, and pride.

While still achieving the intended benefit of expressing emotions, switching from harmful or destructive coping techniques to safer, more productive alternatives can be therapeutic and help with mental health rehabilitation.

Examples of healthier emotional channeling include:

- Creating art (whether it be sculpture, painting, or drawing) is one way to channel negative emotions healthily.

- Dancing (either controlled, disciplined, choreographed dancing, or raucous thrashing to blaring music)

- Singing, listening, creating, and playing an instrument related to music

- Destroying anything in a controlled manner, such as ripping up an old t-shirt or scribbling angrily on paper or in a magazine. • Smashing something, such as breaking big twigs or ice on the ground.

- Writing (everything from fiction to biographies to just rambling on about one's feelings or odd phrases)

- Working out physically (yoga, running, learning a new activity)

- One option is to get a plant and tend to it if you're feeling down.

Channeling is one kind of distraction, but it could be too much to handle when you're already stressed. In such a situation, engaging in less taxing pursuits can serve as a means of passing the time until the unpleasant feelings fade away. Taking part in activities that divert attention away from the sensation of being overwhelmed but still need little concentration can be incredibly helpful.

Here are a few examples:

- Taking a seven-second breath in and eleven-second exhalation

- Keeping track of the number of chair legs in the room

- Having a conversation with a loved one

- Enjoying television

- Taking a stroll outside

- Playing video games

- Napping

- Soaking up in the shower or bath while listening to music you love
- Reading a good book
- Snacking on a hot beverage and a snack
- Window shopping online
- Performing a mental challenge like a puzzle

Coping with Adolescent Feelings

Nothing about being a teenager is realistic. Managing your time between classes, schoolwork, family, and friends may be a real challenge. Trauma and drama are also obstacles that must be overcome.

Your best buddy is ditching you to focus on the next shiny thing, or someone is making false accusations about you online; either way, you're angry and frustrated... again.

You can be losing sleep and noticing changes in your weight because you're so worried about losing "your future" and the pressure to perform better than everyone else.

Or, what can you do when you're a teenager, and the world around you is teeming with possibilities and excitement—but you're feeling nothing but hopelessness and emptiness?

There has to be a method to deal with these wildly fluctuating emotions. The question is, how?

Things to do

Master your feelings.

What the hay! Is it fury? Sad? Feeling irritated? Recognize your emotions and learn to manage them.

Putting those emotions into words helps to alleviate their intensity. Scientists have hypothesized several causes for this phenomenon:

It takes your mind off of things

Emotions can run their course when you give yourself time to identify them. Once you've recognized the emotion, you can take steps to alleviate it.

Being mindful is the practice at hand.

You must first identify your feelings in order to articulate them. This mindfulness method can assist in reducing anxiety and facilitate introspection.

It dispels any uncertainty.

Feelings of negativity can be perplexing. We have an impression, but we can't put our finger on it. When you give your emotions a name, you get insight into both the source of your distress and your emotional response to it. Feeling better is possible with such clarity and acceptance.

Acquire surfing skills

A technique taught in dialectical behavior therapy (DBT), "riding the wave of emotion," is something that therapists who focus on teens often recommend.

Let me explain it to you. We tend to fixate on the specifics of our problems when we're upset, believing that dwelling on them would help us feel better. But this might lead to negative thinking patterns that are hard to break.

In order to let our emotions run their course, we need to disconnect from rational thought and instead immerse ourselves in them.

Release it (in a healthy way)

Attempting to suppress or disregard your emotions can aggravate your problems. A message is being sent to you by your emotions, and you should not disregard it.

Repressing your emotions won't solve the problem; they will remain dormant within you. Keeping your feelings bottled up might lead to physical symptoms like indigestion or worse.

You should get it out of your system for more than just the obvious reason: it has positive health effects! In particular, the "feel-good" hormones oxytocin and endorphins are released into the body when you cry.

They alleviate both mental and bodily discomfort. A good cry will do wonders for your mood.

Some additional methods of emotional release besides having a good cry are:

- Get moving. Try skating, riding your bike, running, surfing, boxing, lifting weights, or anything else that lets out those endorphins and pent-up energy.

- Get down to the music you love. Banging one's head vigorouslyTrusted Going to karaoke or some other fun event where you can let loose and enjoy yourself will help lift your spirits.

- Participate in something you love. To assist you in remembering the happy times and moving on, try doing something entertaining, such as playing a sport, making social media videos, fidgeting with a hobby, or even just playing a game (for a bit!).

- Loosen up. You can allow yourself time to think about and work through your emotions by engaging in a calming activity, such as taking a bath, baking, or even cleaning.

Confronting Challenging Feelings

Some feelings are good. Imagine a world filled with love, joy, curiosity, excitement, thankfulness, and happiness. Feelings like these are wonderful. Sadness, rage, isolation, envy, self-criticism, fear, and rejection are all negative feelings that can be challenging and sometimes unpleasant to deal with.

In instances where we experience unpleasant emotions excessively, intensely, or for an extended period, this becomes very evident. We can learn to cope with negative emotions, no matter how challenging they are. To assist you, I have outlined three stages.

Recognize the Feeling

With practice, you can learn to tune into and name your emotions. Pay attention to your body as much as your emotions. When you're feeling angry, for example, you could notice that your face grows red or that your muscles tighten up.

- Pay attention to your emotions. It can help to identify the emotion you're experiencing when you're feeling bad, like rage. Doing this is far more effective than acting as if you don't feel anything or being angry. For instance: "Ian in my study group drives me crazy!" "I feel envious whenever I see that person with my ex." "I'm terrified every time I have to cross paths with those bullies."

- Determine the source of the emotion. To find out how to deal with your emotions, you need to know where they are coming from.

  - For instance: "Ian always manages to claim credit where it is due whenever we work on group projects."

  - I am reminded of my unresolved feelings for my ex whenever I witness them engaging in flirtatious behavior with other individuals.

  - "It worries me that bullies do what they do to other people, even though they don't pick on me."

- Keep quiet. Being in touch with your feelings and able to articulate them is different from assigning blame. The person who steals your credit may not understand what he's doing, and it's unlikely that your ex is plotting revenge by seeing someone else. Your emotions are a tool for understanding the world around you.

Be okay with feeling whatever you're feeling; it's normal and understandable. You shouldn't be hard on yourself because of how you feel. Experiencing them is natural. Stop being so hard on yourself; accepting your feelings is the first step toward moving forward.

Do Something!

You can choose the best way to communicate your feelings after you've recognized and comprehended them. Having a mental conversation about how you're feeling can be therapeutic at times. Still, there will be other moments when you'd rather take action.

- First, figure out how you'd like to convey your feelings. Should you approach another person with tact and diplomacy? Have a conversation with a friend about it? Alternatively, try going for a run to burn off some steam. As an illustration:
  - I need to keep out of another sticky situation where Ian takes charge of a project, but venting my frustrations to him won't help.
  - Around my ex, I will keep my head held high. Subsequently, I intend to play some melancholy music, have a nice cry in solitude, and ultimately release my pain.

- I will inform a school counselor about the situation with the bullies.

- Master the art of mood manipulation. Even if you're not in the mood, make an effort to do what brings you joy. For instance, following a breakup, you might not feel like going out. But getting out of that funk might be as simple as going for a stroll or as involved as watching a hilarious movie with pals.

- Foster a state of contentment. Always remember to be grateful for everything, no matter how small. Something like how good the salad you made for lunch is or how much praise a parent gave you for fixing the Wi-Fi may be it. Even when you're down in the dumps, it can help to keep your focus on the wonderful things around you.

- Seek out assistance. Share your feelings with an adult you trust, such as a parent or a trusted friend. This might provide you with a new perspective while also assisting you in exploring your feelings.

- Get moving. When you work out, your brain releases feel-good endorphins and other feel-good compounds. Physical activity has additional stress-relieving and mood-boosting benefits.

Finally, seek assistance when dealing with challenging emotions.

There will be moments when you can't seem to get over a particularly difficult feeling. Additional support may be necessary if you experience persistent feelings of melancholy or anxiety for longer than two weeks or if your emotions are so intense that you consider harming yourself or others.

Seek immediate assistance from an adult you trust, such as a parent, guidance counselor, instructor, or coach. Get in touch with a helpline operator if you are in a situation where you do not have access to an adult.

Classifying and naming feelings

Everyday life includes describing our emotions, but the words we use to do so typically originate in our adolescent years.

What is the best way to express that you're not feeling well or that you're not "myself" today? Saying something like "my head's sore" might lead you to the root of the problem. "I was feeling stressed last night, so I didn't sleep well," you might claim.

A person's emotional and mental states are the most fundamental descriptions of who they are. The degree to which you are able to identify, categorize, and use them is indicative of your emotional and social literacy.

Indeed, socio-emotional literacy is the subject of entire academic departments.

Feelings, when considered in isolation, are similar to the sight words your adolescent learned in kindergarten; however, instead of and, it, is, and look, most students learn happy, furious, sad, and a host of other emotions. I guess that's about all.

Let's go back to the first. Even though we experience emotions constantly, our educational system manages to exclude teaching students how to identify and manage their emotions in favor of imparting less relevant knowledge. (As for me, I still haven't gotten around to dissecting another worm or reviewing the Pythagorean theorem; maybe you have.)

Emotions are important because they serve as signals for our values, how we interpret an event, what we require, and what we prefer or detest. But emotions can be difficult and unpleasant, so we try to bury them. Maybe we were told we shouldn't talk about our feelings when we were younger, so we do the same.

This might work temporarily, but in the long run, repressed emotions will find a way to surface. Problems with physical or mental health can manifest in a variety of ways, for example, gastrointestinal issues, fibromyalgia, anxiety, depression, or phobias.

When we are oblivious to our feelings, it is impossible to control them or get our needs addressed. In order to have a deeper comprehension of your feelings, consider the following four suggestions.

A guide to recognizing emotions

Please take note that feelings and emotions are distinct concepts. They are often used interchangeably in everyday speech, so I will also be doing that in this post.

Feelings
Word List

Happy
Adored
Alive
Appreciated
Cheerful
Ecstatic
Excited
Grateful
Glad
Hopeful
Jolly
Jovial
Joyful
Loved
Merry
Optimistic
Pleased
Satisfied
Tender
Terrific
Thankful
Uplifted
Warm

Mad
Aggravated
Accused
Angry
Bitter
Cross
Defensive
Frustrated
Furious
Hostile
Impatient
Infuriated
Insulted
Jaded
Offended
Ornery
Outraged
Pestered
Rebellious
Resistant
Revengeful
Scorned
Spiteful
Testy
Used
Violated

Sad
Alone
Blue
Burdened
Depressed
Devastated
Disappointed
Discouraged
Grief-stricken
Gloomy
Hopeless
Let down
Lonely
Heartbroken
Melancholy
Miserable
Neglected
Pessimistic
Remorseful
Resentful
Solemn
Threatened

Scared
Afraid
Alarmed
Anxious
Bashful
Cautious
Fearful
Frightened
Horrified
Lost
Haunted
Helpless
Hesitant
Insecure
Nervous
Petrified
Puzzled
Reassured
Reserved
Sheepish
Tearful
Uncomfortable
Useless

Surprise
Astonished
Curious
Delighted
Enchanted
Exhilarated
Incredulous
Inquisitive
Impressed
Mystified
Passionate
Playful
Replenished
Splendid
Shocked
Stunned

Disgust
Embarrassed
Exposed
Guilty
Ignored
Inadequate
Incompetent
Inhibited
Inept
Inferior
Insignificant
Sick
Shame
Squashed
Stupid
Ugly
Unaccepted

What is my emotional state?

Words like "good," "fine," and "okay" do not represent feelings. The first step is to sit quietly for a while and pay attention to your emotions. Be open-minded and watch what happens. Feelings are feelings; they are neither good nor negative. Pay attention to your feelings without constantly judging yourself or offering advice on how you should or should not be feeling. If you're having trouble figuring out what emotion you're experiencing, you're not alone; making a feelings list can be helpful. I am lonely, for instance.

2. In what parts of my body is it most noticeable?

To further connect with this emotion, pay attention to where it occurs in your body. When we become aware of an unpleasant emotion, we may try to divert our attention away from it because it isn't easy to feel. Here is a chance to go more into it. I may feel the isolation in my chest, for instance.

If you're still having trouble putting a name to the feeling, this can serve as a good jumping-off place. Look over your entire body, from head to toe, and focus on any places where you feel tightness or stress. What could that physical feeling indicate?

A lump in the throat, for instance, could be a sign that you're feeling down in the dumps. Clenched fists and stooped shoulders are signs of rage and tension, respectively.

Remember that we can experience multiple emotions simultaneously. For example, when faced with a new problem, we may experience a mix of emotions, from relief to sadness.

3. What gives me this sensation?

One deceptive thing about emotions is that they aren't always logical. The source of our emotional reaction may be anything from our history or something related to the here and now. Another possible source of emotion is how you interpret a certain person or circumstance. Anger is a common emotion that can accompany the perception of rudeness.

Just keep sitting with the experience and trying to piece together what happened to make you feel this way. For instance, I'm home alone, feeling lonely since my friends all have plans for the evening.

Because our thoughts have an effect on our emotions, being aware of our thoughts could help us understand why we are feeling a particular way. For instance, I'm feeling despondent despite my earlier assurance that today would be a terrible day.

There's no need to stress if you're still confused. Your feelings are real and important, regardless of whether they are fully conscious or not. Keep watching it without passing judgment.

4. What am I going to require?

Continue to be present with the emotion or emotions, pay attention to where they are coming from, try to understand why they are there, and figure out what will assist right now. For instance, I should make an effort to be more thoughtful toward myself and plan ahead of time.

The caveat is that you can't help but feel the bad emotions before you can overcome them. We try to avoid dealing with our emotions by focusing on other things, on our accomplishments, and other people. Still, ultimately, only we can control our own feelings. Emotional literacy is a skill that requires constant work, so permit yourself to be patient. Being able to put a name to your emotions will help you respond more effectively rather than react.

This isn't very good. Why should I care about how I feel?

It can be quite unpleasant for some time. But as we let go of our feelings, we let go of the control we believe they have over us as well. We have the power to heal from previous wounds, strengthen our bonds, and experience life to the fullest.

If we put off dealing with our feelings, we could go for solace in things other than ourselves. Even worse, we risk fooling ourselves into thinking that we will finally be happy "when."

"I can relax when I have my credit card paid off."

"I'll feel safe when I have a loving partner."

"I'll be confident when I lose that weight."

Our emotions accompany us wherever we go; thus, no matter how well-planned our lives are, we will inevitably experience anxious, fearful, and insecure sentiments. No matter how briefly an effect it has, we keep looking for anything new to "make us feel better," and eventually, we go back to square one.

What makes feeling our emotions so difficult (and appealing) is that there is no way out except through. Good and terrible emotions alike, though, are transitory and will eventually fade. Having a strong support system, practicing self-compassion, and seeing a therapist can be incredibly helpful when dealing with these intense feelings.

The link between mental processes, feelings, and actions

Sometimes, it's hard to make sense of your emotions and thoughts, even after listening to all the advice from the UCC, friends, parents, and social media. That's the norm. A worldwide crisis has disturbed "normalcy," and it is normal to feel affected by this. Everyone does that sometimes. Still, it may be possible to keep finding little joy in the face of fresh difficulties by controlling and rephrasing some persistent and distracting ideas.

When you find yourself overcome by negative ideas and strong emotions, consider one of these many ways of reframing.

Determine the nature of your emotions and the factors that are impacting them:

Perhaps you are experiencing difficulties with a school project, or perhaps a much-anticipated event has been postponed. Then the crushing realization hits: "I'll never see my friends again" or "I have no future." Feelings, what are they? Which actions follow?

Keeping a journal or other "thought record" in which you jot down your answers to these questions might be helpful. It could also help to challenge some of your assumptions.

- ♦ How plausible is this idea?
- ♦ Is this idea grounded in logic or emotion?
- ♦ How can I back up this theory with evidence?
- ♦ Could this evidence have different meanings?

- Because there is more nuance to this scenario than meets the eye, am I seeing it in a simplistic light?

- Is there another way of thinking about this that is more grounded in reality and would be less stressful?

Switch to a more descriptive mode of thinking:

"Everything is horrible" is an easy way to think, but shifting from a binary to a more descriptive mindset might be more beneficial. Being stuck at home could be a lot of things, including a letdown and an annoyance. The situation may be dire, but it's probably not that bad. Reconnect with the good things in your life and the chances you've been given. It may be easier to control the need to react hastily to dire situations if you surround yourself with things that pique your interest.

Embrace change and shift your focus from demands to preferences:

A game-changer is to adjust your expectations of yourself, other people, and your circumstances. If you think everything will work out the way you want it to, you might be in for some disappointment. Once again, make use of receptivity and interest.

Realize your preferences and distinguish between needs and wishes. A person's physical and mental health, as well as their ability to stay alive, depend on their needs. While access to healthy food is essential, dining out is a luxury.

Concentrate on the power you possess:

Change your perspective from that of a helpless victim to that of a powerful creator. If you want to prevent spreading the illness and keep doctors and nurses from becoming overloaded, staying home is the way to go. Take a moment to reflect on how you may be of service to others, whether it's by pitching in to help out around the house, lending a hand to a fellow student, or offering your time to a local group that promotes health and wellness. Even if you can't control everything that happens, you can control your reaction.

Our emotions and actions are influenced by the automatic thoughts that arise in every given situation. Feelings of melancholy, rage, anxiety, and annoyance might set in when our automatic thoughts are unpleasant. It can be challenging to finish coursework and have positive social relationships when these emotions lead to undesirable habits.

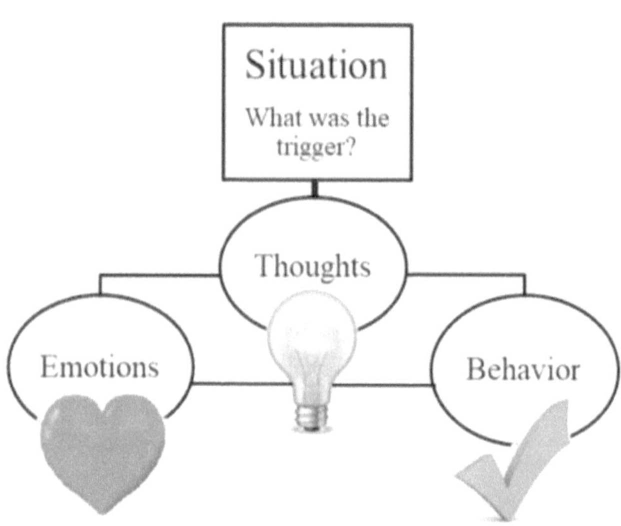

CHAPTER 3

Building the Foundation: Core CBT Skills

Developmentally, the adolescent years are crucial. Depression symptoms, including melancholy and hopelessness, are reported by one-third of high school pupils, according to experts, suggesting that mental health issues are frequent during this time. Teens, like adults, may find that therapy is an effective means of coping with these and other common issues.

Treatment options for teenagers are diverse and may include a variety of therapeutic approaches. You should educate yourself on your alternatives and the processes involved in each form of therapy for your adolescent so that you can make an informed decision.

A foundational overview of cognitive behavioral therapy

As a kind of talk therapy, cognitive behavioral therapy (CBT) is widely used. Cognitive behavioral therapy (CBT) is usually designed as a short-term treatment, with improvements typically shown after a few weeks to a few months, unlike some other therapies.

While it is important to consider your history, cognitive behavioral therapy (CBT) primarily aims to help you address your present challenges. And many paths to that goal involve this form of treatment.

How Does CBT for Adolescents and Young Adults Operate?

In counseling for children, the majority of the therapeutic work is typically with the parents or guardians, showing them how to apply cognitive behavioral therapy (CBT) techniques with their child.

When working with adolescents and older children, the therapist and caretaker work together to teach the patient and caretaker new skills for dealing with the problems that first prompted them to seek help. With the support of caregivers, this procedure places greater agency in the hands of the client, allowing them to make informed decisions about their treatment even when they are not in therapy.

How Can CBT Benefit Children and Adolescents?

Anxiety, sadness, low self-esteem, problems with identity, and behavioral disorders are just a few of the many mental health conditions that cognitive behavioral therapy can help with. Despite the fact that CBT needs some tweaks to be more effective with teenagers, a mountain of evidence indicates that it's a great tool to have on hand when dealing with this demographic.

Among the most prevalent uses of CBT with youths are the following:

The following conditions can benefit from cognitive behavioral therapy:

- ◆ anxiety, panic attacks,

♦ social anxiety,

♦ depression,

♦ attention deficit hyperactivity disorder,

♦ obsessive-compulsive disorder,

♦ eating disorders,

♦ insomnia.

Methods of Cognitive Behavioral Therapy for Kids

Children can benefit from cognitive behavioral therapy (CBT) in many different ways, including:

♦ One of the most researched forms of cognitive behavioral therapy (CBT) and the most beneficial, especially for teenagers suffering from anxiety, is individual CBT, which entails meetings with a professional therapist one-on-one.

♦ Group and individual sessions of Parent-Child CBT are available. Children who have experienced trauma or abuse are better able to heal, and parents who have struggled to learn to control their emotions and raise resilient children benefit greatly from this program.

♦ Improved communication and support within the family can be achieved through family-based cognitive behavioral therapy (CBT), which involves incorporating family therapy into cognitive behavioral treatment for children.

♦ Cognitive Behavioral Therapy (CBT) in a group setting: CBT taught in a group with children of the same age helps kids learn valuable skills while also boosting their confidence.

♦ Trauma-focused cognitive behavioral therapy (TF-CBT): TF-CBT has a strong track record of success in assisting traumatized children and teens, as well as their caretakers, in experiencing recovery. This is especially true when the treatment plan is adjusted according to the child's developmental level.

♦ Cognitive behavioral therapy (CBT) combined with motivational enhancement therapy (MET): This treatment combination is highly beneficial in helping adolescents who are struggling with substance use disorders. This method of treatment is based on Motivational Interviewing technique.

What follows is an overview of cognitive behavioral therapy (CBT) methods, the problems they target, and the outcomes patients might anticipate from CBT.

When doing CBT, what methods are utilized?

Central to cognitive behavioral therapy (CBT) is the idea that how you think influences your feelings, which influence your actions.

For instance, CBT stresses the need to recognize the chain reaction between negative ideas, emotions, and behaviors. Changing the way you think about things can have a good effect on your emotions and actions.

You will learn practical, immediately applicable skills from your therapist. These are lifelong abilities that will serve you well.

There are various approaches to cognitive behavioral therapy (CBT), each tailored to a specific problem and set of objectives. No matter what method your therapist uses, you can expect to work on the following:

♦ Recognizing and naming problematic thought patterns and their effects on your life

♦ Recognizing negative thought patterns and learning to reframe them in a way that improves your mood

♦ Learning and implementing new behaviors

Your therapist will determine the most effective cognitive behavioral therapy (CBT) procedures after consultation with you and gathering information about the problem you wish to address.

The following nine tactics are among the most common forms of cognitive behavioral therapy (CBT):

1. Mental reorganization or rethinking

To do this, one must examine destructive ways of thinking critically.

Or maybe you have a tendency to generalize too much, think the worst, or fixate on insignificant details. Your actions are influenced by your thoughts, and they can even come true.

In order to help you recognize destructive patterns of thinking, your therapist will ask you to describe how you process particular scenarios. Once you become aware of them, you may train yourself to think more constructively and optimistically.

"That report wasn't my best work, but I'm a valuable employee, and I contribute in many ways." This is a much better alternative than "I blew the report because I'm totally useless."

2. Discovery with guidance

The therapist will get to know your perspective throughout guided discovery. The next step is for them to pose questions that will force you to reevaluate your assumptions and views.

Both evidence that supports and evidence that contradicts your assumptions may be requested of you.

While doing so, you will broaden your horizons and think about topics in ways you never have before. Doing so can lead you down a more beneficial road.

3. Trained eye contact

Fears and phobias can be overcome through exposure treatment. Your therapist will help you face your fears and anxieties by introducing you to the things that make you anxious and then teaching you techniques to deal with those things when they arise.

Doing something in little bits is possible. Over time, being exposed to new situations might help you become more resilient and self-assured.

4. Documenting thoughts and journaling

An age-old practice, writing helps one connect with one's inner ideas.

In order to help your therapist identify negative thoughts that may have occurred to you in between sessions, they may ask you to write them down along with positive alternatives.

As an additional writing activity, record any new ideas or actions you've implemented since our last session. You can better appreciate your progress when you put it in writing.

5. Activating behaviors and arranging activities

Putting something in your schedule could help you do it, especially if you have a fear of or avoidance of doing it otherwise. Making a decision is easier when you don't have to think about it.

Making a routine out of your activities allows you to put what you've learned into practice and helps you form positive habits.

6. Experiments on behavior

Anxiety disorders characterized by catastrophic thought are commonly studied using behavioral tests.

Predicting what's going to happen is the first step before doing something that usually makes you nervous. You will discuss whether or not the forecast was accurate later on.

The likelihood of the projected disaster becoming a reality may begin to diminish with time. You should probably ease into more challenging activities and work your way up.

7. Strategies for calming the mind and reducing stress

When you participate in cognitive behavioral therapy, you may learn progressive relaxation techniques like:

- deep breathing exercises

- muscular relaxing

- Visuals

Lessen your anxiety and feel more in charge of your life with the practical tools you'll learn. If you suffer from social anxiety, phobias, or any other kind of stress, this may assist.

8. Playing the part

One way to prepare for challenging situations is to play the part of a character. Avoiding scary circumstances is just one of many benefits of role-playing, which also helps with the following:

- developing problem-solving abilities

- building comfort and self-assurance in specific settings

- honing social skills

- training for assertiveness

- enhancing communication abilities

9. Approximating successively

Doing so entails dividing large projects into smaller, more manageable ones. Your self-assurance grows gradually as you go along since each stage builds on the one before it.

During a cognitive behavioral therapy session, what exactly takes place?

During your initial appointment, you will assist the therapist in comprehending your issue and your objectives for cognitive behavioral therapy (CBT). Next, the therapist will establish a course of action to reach the desired outcome.

Objectives ought to be:

♦ Specific

♦ Measurable

♦ Achievable

♦ Realistic

♦ Time-bound

Group, family, or individual treatment may be suggested by the therapist, depending on your circumstances and SMART objectives.

The frequency and duration of sessions can vary from week to week based on the client's needs and availability, but they typically run around an hour.

As part of the process, you will also be requested to complete worksheets, keep a journal, or complete specific assignments in between sessions.

It is crucial to feel comfortable talking to your therapist and to communicate openly with them. If you aren't feeling totally at ease with your current therapist, look for someone else whom you can relate to and confide in more readily.

Try to find a therapist who specializes in cognitive behavioral therapy (CBT) and has worked with clients like you before. Verify if they have the necessary licenses and certifications.

Seek advice from medical professionals you trust, such as your doctor or nurse. Medical doctors, psychologists, social workers, psychiatric nurse practitioners, marriage and family therapists, and anyone who has completed training in mental health may all be considered practitioners.

It usually takes a few weeks to a few months for cognitive behavioral therapy (CBT) to start working.

How might cognitive behavioral therapy be of assistance?

Cognitive behavioral therapy (CBT) is useful for a wide range of common issues, including anxiety, learning to manage stressful situations, and more.

Cognitive behavioral therapy (CBT) can help even in the absence of a formal medical diagnosis.

Additionally, it can be useful for:

- learning to control intense feelings like anger, anxiety, or sadness

- coping with loss

- reducing the impact of mental illness symptoms or avoiding relapses

- dealing with physical health issues

- resolving conflicts

- enhancing communication abilities

- training in assertiveness

Whether used alone or in conjunction with other treatments, CBT has the potential to alleviate symptoms of many different medical issues. In this category, you will find conditions such as:

- addictions

- anxiety disorders

- bipolar illness

- chronic pain

- Mood disorders

Some examples of mental health issues include:
- eating disorders,

- phobias,

- PTSD,

- schizophrenia,

- sexual problems,

- sleep difficulties,

- tinnitus.

Case in point:

Cognitive Behavioral Therapy for Children Facing Divorce

The 12-year-old Allie's parents are divorcing. Troubles have been piling up for Allie both at home and in the classroom. She refuses to turn in her homework and is being combative. She is typically a respectful and diligent student, but her parents are worried about her behavior. Her parents think it would be best if she saw a therapist. Allie opens up to her therapist after a few sessions about how her parents' divorce has affected her and how angry she is with them for severing her family. A therapist explains to Allie's parents that their daughter's behavioral problems stem from an adjustment disorder that she developed as a result of the recent changes in their family dynamic.

The therapist guides Allie through cognitive restructuring exercises designed to open her mind to new perspectives on her current predicament. Her parents have found happiness, and they continue to love and support her. They hope that she finds happiness, too.

The therapist also works with the parents to create a plan for discipline that will assist their children in replacing negative habits with more desirable ones. Allie and her therapist focused on recognizing destructive beliefs and finding healthy methods to express her feelings for four months. As Allie starts submitting her assignments on time, her grades start to rise. Eventually, Allie finds happiness again once she learns to embrace her evolving family.

CBT for Adolescents with ADHD

A sixteen-year-old named Cam is a high school student. He is uninspired and sluggish, according to his dad. Because of his low grades, he is afraid he will not have enough to get into college after high school. In spite of his strong exam scores, Cam has a hard time with homework and long projects. Teachers have called Cam's dad many times to discuss his student's conduct in class. During class, he allegedly doesn't pay attention and even interrupts other pupils.

Dad brings Cam to a psychiatrist, who says he has attention deficit hyperactivity disorder. To help with his behavioral troubles, Cam is prescribed medicine by the psychiatrist, who also recommends that he see a CBT therapist.

Cam finds success in treatment when he learns to prioritize his objectives and divide them into manageable chunks. Following his success in using a planner to keep track of assignments and due dates, he applies this skill to his homework and starts turning things in on time.

In addition, he improves his interactions with instructors and classmates by learning social skills. After six months of treatment, Cam's grades improved dramatically, and he is ready to start applying to colleges. His father has also seen a shift in his son's conduct at home, remarking that Cam is now more cooperative and less disruptive.

Can Children and Teens Rely on Cognitive Behavioral Therapy?

Cognitive behavioral therapy (CBT) has been the subject of a great deal of study regarding its efficacy in adults. Still, its use with children has received far less attention.

However, recent research on the topic has shown that cognitive behavioral therapy (CBT) is highly effective when used with youth. There seems to be substantial data indicating that CBT is a successful therapy method for children. Yet, additional study is necessary to delve further into these results.

Adolescents diagnosed with anxiety and depression can benefit from cognitive behavioral therapy (CBT) when given the proper environment and guided by an experienced therapist, according to a study done by the National Institute of Health (NIH).

In addition to treating anxiety and depression, CBT is beneficial in treating PTSD and disruptive behavior disorder in children, according to the CDC.

Additional studies have shown that cognitive behavioral therapy (CBT) is beneficial in treating a variety of illnesses in children, such as substance use disorders, bullying, self-esteem issues, eating disorders, and bedwetting.

Do you see any dangers?

CBT is typically thought of as a safe therapy; nonetheless, there are a few considerations to bear in mind:

- Some people may initially find it difficult or unpleasant to face their difficulties head-on; however, this varies from person to person.

- Exposure treatment and other forms of cognitive behavioral therapy (CBT) can exacerbate anxiety and stress levels as they progress.

- You won't see results right away. It requires dedication and perseverance to practice new skills in the time between therapy sessions and even after treatment has been completed. Consider cognitive behavioral therapy (CBT) as a permanent adjustment to your way of life that you want to maintain and even enhance over time.

Three Home CBT Activities for Children and Teens

One of the most prevalent concerns that children and teens bring to therapy is anxiety, which can often be accompanied by other diseases or challenges. Here are some relaxation techniques that can assist your child in managing stress and anxiety.

1. Exercise for Deep Breathing

A plethora of easy-to-follow, at-home deep breathing exercises are available.

For a home-based deep breathing exercise:

- Hold your nose open for five seconds while you breathe in.

- Breathe deeply into your belly button for five seconds.

♦ Count to five while exhaling through your lips.

♦ Continue.

If you suffer from social anxiety and want to find a way to relax without drawing attention to yourself, try practicing this approach for 5–10 minutes at a time.

2. A Practice in Grounding

This imagery-guided grounding practice can help alleviate anxiety, in addition to bringing your attention back to the present moment through the utilization of sensory input from your immediate surroundings:

Imagine a relaxing spot to start. There must be a special place in your home, a beloved site, a beach, or perhaps a recollection of your youth. Give yourself five to ten minutes to fully immerse yourself in the mental image of this location.

Put your five senses to work by inquiring about:

1. One, what are you seeing? Take in your environment by looking at this room. What does the faraway horizon look like? Looking around you, what do you notice? Make an effort to pay attention to information you might otherwise overlook.

2. Have you heard anything? Take careful note of all the sounds around you. Do you notice faint or loud sounds? How far away are they, if at all?

3. What flavors are there? What are you now consuming? Is that the case? If so, how does it taste? Is it savory or sweet?

4. How are you feeling? What temperature is it? Can you feel the wind? Are the sunbeams hitting your skin and making you feel warmer? Is a warm blanket covering you instead? Keep your focus on the sensations.

5. What scents are present? How does this place smell? Is it a strong or subtle aroma? Pay close attention to and enjoy the aromas you detect.

If you find yourself mentally tense, try this practice. Take as much time as you need to imagine yourself in your cozy home. Make it a point to feel secure and at peace.

3. A Technique for Gradual Muscle Relaxation

The progressive muscle relaxation exercise is a simple at-home technique for relaxing tense muscles:

1. Foot: Bring your toes together in a tight curl, maintain for five seconds, and then let go.

2. Step two: calves. Point your toes, hold for five seconds, and then let go.

3. Step three: thighs bring your thighs together in a tight squeeze, maintain for five seconds, and then let go.

4. In the fourth position, the torso, tighten your abdominal muscles for five seconds before releasing them.

5. Five, for your back, bring your shoulder blades together in a squeeze and hold for five seconds before releasing.

6. Shoulders: Pull your shoulder blades in toward your ears, pull them together, and hold for 5 seconds. Lower them back down.

7. For the arms, you should clench your muscles by bending them in such a way that your forearm is touching your biceps; keep this position for five seconds before releasing.

8. For the hands, curl your fingers into your palms to form a tight fist. Hold for five seconds, and then let go.

9. Draw your features in toward the middle of your face and scrunch them up; hold for five seconds, then let go.

10. Full body: simultaneously tense and squeeze every muscle in your body, hold for 5 seconds, and then release.

If you suffer from anxiety-related muscle tightness, try doing this relaxation technique every day.

Improving one's way of thinking

Now, let's discuss your remarkable mind. Good mental health is essential for a fulfilling existence; one must know the difference between thought and thinking and must also accept that the mind generates fiction rather than fact.

Most of us tend to believe whatever story (or idea, I'll use both words interchangeably) our minds conjure up, latch on to it, and engage in an internal monologue with it. Countless heartaches may result from this. For instance, recognize that negative self-talk like "I am not good enough" or "I am stupid" is a tale and not the reality when it arises. Probably one that you have internalized from a long ago when someone else told you.

No matter how much space there is, our minds will constantly generate new ideas. It tries to make sense of the world by coming up with all sorts of stories. Some are helpful, and some that aren't. Your task is to train your brain to accept certain narratives as true and reject others. By training your brain to ignore negative thoughts and focus on positive ones, you can train it to think more productively.

In this approach, you may train your brain to think for yourself rather than the other way around. You develop the ability to differentiate between your first idea and the subsequent steps in your cognitive process. You can't change your first impression. But after that, you have a ton of power over your thinking process and how you react to that initial concept.

Many people believe that logotherapy's creator, Victor Frankl, said the following. "In the space between stimulus and response lies our growth and our freedom," it adds. The need to change one's mindset from reactive to proactive is aptly captured in this phrase.

Locate the empty space between the stimuli and your answer; this will help you avoid being automatically hooked into your first thinking, which is the stimulus. You may consciously determine if this is a helpful notion or if it's better to let it go by using that space.

Consider the following scenario: "I am a loser" is your initial thought. Instead of reacting mechanically, try to find the empty space that follows this notion. If you want to make a smart choice, take a moment to reflect on whether responding to this negative thinking will help or if you'd be better off letting it go.

After you've made the positive decision to ignore it, you may take it a step further by telling yourself a supportive tale, such as, "I want to lose weight and be as healthy as possible; at the same time, I choose to accept and love myself the way I am right now." It makes no difference to me.

Whether you realize it or not, you are constantly reinforcing thoughts since you control your brain. Make an effort and train your mind to think positively if you want to succeed.

In other words, throughout the next week, try to become an empathetic, curious, and nonjudgmental observer of your thought process. Pay attention to which thoughts arise that are heavily tied emotionally.

Jot down your ideas while keeping in mind that they are only stories, not facts, and that they don't reflect you in any way. Just think of them as automatic brain reflexes. You might even start to wonder where those ideas originate. To rephrase, who has previously spoken these exact words to you?

CHAPTER 4

Embracing Balance: Core DBT Skills

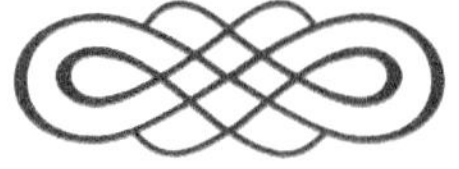

Due to the unique issues that teens face in this vital era of development, DBT is especially relevant for them. Peer pressure, growing independence, and a maelstrom of emotions characterize adolescence.

Emotional control, self-esteem, self-identity, and stress management are all areas where teenagers may face challenges. Through DBT, individuals are given the necessary tools to overcome these obstacles.

The four pillars of dialectical behavior therapy (DBT) are interpersonal effectiveness, emotional regulation, distress tolerance, and mindfulness.

Teens who have mastered these abilities are better able to control their feelings, deal with stress, build stronger relationships, and make wiser choices in life.

They become more self-aware by learning to identify and tolerate their feelings without criticism.

Is DBT What It Claims To Be?

One form of talk therapy is dialectical behavior therapy (DBT), which holds that people have problems for a variety of reasons, including their biology, their skill set, and the amount of invalidation they've experienced. Teens succeed with DBT because it teaches them skills and gives them validation and support.

Differentiating dialectical behavior therapy (DBT) from other therapies is its emphasis on both acceptance and transformation rather than just one or the other. This middle ground between resistance and openness gives people the encouragement and guidance they need to acquire the knowledge and abilities they lack.

Skills training, individual treatment, phone coaching, and therapy consultation sessions were all part of the original dialectical behavior therapy model:

- People learn how to change through skills training. Individual therapy helps with skill development, gives time to fix learning problems, validates feelings, and models good relationships.

- Short phone calls called "coaching" can help clients employ skills in the here and now, and therapist consultations allow therapists to talk about clients' problems and make sure they're giving the finest treatment possible.

Nevertheless, DBT has been effectively adapted for various people and contexts. The therapist will give orientation papers that cover their specific dialectical behavior therapy program before starting a new client on the program.

Why Is Dialectical Behavior Therapy Modified for Adolescents?

There is a research-validated program called DBT-A that caters to the unique needs of adolescents, as it differs significantly from DBT for adults (DBT for Adolescents).

Healthcare Providers' Role

The involvement of caregivers is the most notable distinction in dialectical behavior therapy (DBT) for teenagers. Caregivers often participate in skill training with patients or receive specialized instruction in their role. Caregivers will also have the opportunity to participate in individual treatment sessions or join in on extra family sessions as needed. Not only does the teen receive phone coaching from the therapist, but so do the caretakers. A key component of maximizing development is the involvement of caregivers.

Embarking on the Middle Path: DBT Skills for Teens

The Walking the Middle Path skill module is a new addition to the skill training rotation in dialectical behavior therapy (DBT) for teenagers. When problems emerge at home, they might be a barrier to treatment, but Walking the Middle Path helps with that. Dialectics, validation, and behavior modification are the focal points of this unit's curriculum. Putting an emphasis on these abilities equips caregivers and their adolescents with the tools necessary to reduce conflict. When families have a shared language, they are better able to communicate and resolve conflicts.

Reflection on Growing Older

Additionally, the developmental stage of the teenager must be considered in DBT therapy for teens. Group therapy sessions for adolescents are typically shorter than those for adults in order to cater to the younger clientele's shorter attention span.

The use of metaphors and examples, as well as more physical touch, may characterize some forms of group and individual treatment. Good therapists will also know that adult developmental tasks are different from teenage developmental tasks and will be able to use this knowledge to help their clients.

Adolescent Dialectical Behavior Therapy (DBT) Approaches

Because every youngster is unique, dialectical behavior therapy (DBT) has evolved to accommodate a wide range of treatment modalities. The levels of care vary from very low in a classroom setting to very high in a hospital setting to ensure patient safety and everything in between. Determining an appropriate degree of care for an adolescent can be helped by consulting with a therapist or psychiatrist.

Directed behavior therapy for outpatients

Although there are other possible approaches, the most popular and conventional kind of dialectical behavior therapy (DBT) is outpatient therapy. If a person does not fare well in a group setting or if the organization does not provide groups, they may be able to learn new skills in individual therapy.

Individual therapy, skill-building groups, and phone coaching are all components of the entire concept that may be offered through outpatient therapy. Apps or online dialectical behavior therapy (DBT) alternatives may be integrated when new technology is being created. Teens who are having difficulty but are functional and secure enough in their peer groups to not require more intensive treatment at a facility like the ones below may benefit from outpatient therapy.

Dialectical Behavior Therapy for Intensive Outpatients

Group sessions for intensive outpatient therapy typically occur three to five times weekly. Outpatient treatment may include some or all dialectical behavior therapy (DBT), depending on the program. There may be more review, processing, and troubleshooting in intensive outpatient therapy groups due to the higher group frequency, and skills may be covered more than once or more quickly. People who are about to be hospitalized or who are leaving a more intensive level of care often participate in intensive outpatient therapy.

Both outpatient and residential treatment options

Because adolescents in residential and inpatient treatment programs are present all day, there are several opportunities for creative and varied delivery of dialectical behavior therapy. A teenager may have the opportunity to learn all of the DBT skills in the course of their residential program, albeit this does depend on the program's duration and structure.

A residential program may also opt to narrow their skill set to a manageable level, with the goal of making sure the client is able to apply what they've learned even when they're not in the program. Treatment in residential facilities often also includes individual therapy. Interactions with personnel, behavior management, and indirect influence on other groups are likely to be offered by DBT.

Although inpatient treatment is often shorter than residential treatment, it will nevertheless significantly alter dialectical behavior therapy (DBT). It is common for inpatient programs to employ a more condensed version of dialectical behavior therapy (DBT) with an emphasis on distress tolerance and emotion regulation. It is important to reinforce the exposure to dialectical behavior therapy (DBT) in the inpatient context with outpatient treatment following hospital discharge since the inpatient setting is more of a "boot camp" approach.

Cognitive Impairment and DBT

People with cognitive impairments sometimes have a hard time finding effective treatment options; DBT has been modified to address this need. A skilled therapist can make additional modifications to accommodate a teen's needs, even though the adoption was originally created for adults with cognitive limitations.

For better comprehension, the terminology and treatment plan have been condensed. Some of the changes include the addition of more pictures, simpler language, and more appealing worksheets. Different learning styles are also taken into account while modifying the group's structure.

Behavior Modification Programs in Educational Institutions

Classes or groups utilizing dialectical behavior therapy (DBT) STEPS-A are increasingly being offered in schools. There is no clinical component to the school program. Everyone who could use the skills, regardless of whether they have a mental health diagnosis or not, is welcome in a non-clinical program.

Anyone, not just clinicians, can administer the skills-based school program, which does away with dialectical behavior therapy's other features. Nonetheless, a DBT program comparable to the outpatient approaches may be available at some schools that have therapists on staff.

Teens DBT Skills and Common Techniques

While the specific dialectical behavior therapy (DBT) approaches utilized with adolescents may differ from program to program, there are a number of tools and techniques that are commonly used. Techniques used in teenage programs are a combination of those central to dialectical behavior therapy (DBT) and those specifically relevant to working with this age group.

With teenagers, some of the most prevalent DBT skills and approaches include:

1. Being fully present or practicing awareness
2. interpersonal effectiveness, or engaging in more fulfilling human interactions;
3. distress tolerance, or responding less frequently or with less intensity to distress

4. the ability to identify and manage one's emotional states

Being present

An essential skill in dialectical behavior therapy (DBT) is mindfulness, which can improve your ability to deal with stressful situations.

To practice mindfulness is to pay close attention to the present moment. It aids in avoiding preoccupation with the past and future.

Learn more about yourself, your desires, and emotional and mental regulation with the use of mindfulness skills in dialectical behavior therapy (DBT).

The "what" and "how" skills are the two main categories of mindfulness-based dialectical behavior therapy (DBT).

"What skills?" are the actions you do to manage difficult situations. Among them are:

Three ways to be an observer are:
- not identifying what happens;
- putting what you see into words;
- actively engaging in what you see.

When it comes to coping, the "how" abilities are all about the mechanics. Among them are:
- Challenge negative self-talk and thoughts in a non-judgmental way.
- Concentrating on a single task at a time

- When you do what helps you rather than what you believe is proper, you are operating efficiently.

An equilibrium between emotion and reason, or a "wise mind," is what one aspires to cultivate through mindfulness training.

Maximizing efficiency in interpersonal interactions

The goal of the dialectical behavior therapy (DBT) skillset known as "interpersonal effectiveness" is to assist clients in developing and sustaining positive connections with one another. Developing these abilities can help you respect yourself, establish healthy boundaries, and advocate for your own needs.

One interpersonal effectiveness ability that might help you take care of yourself and express your true desires is learning to say no.

The ability to effectively interact with people serves three primary purposes:

- Connection effectiveness: enhancing and sustaining relationships

- Objective effectiveness: achieving one's goals

- Self-esteem effectiveness: helping one to value and respect oneself

Tolerance for emotional distress

Another basic skill in dialectical behavior therapy (DBT) that can help you deal with unpleasant situations is distress tolerance. When dealing with emotional distress, it is important to employ healthy coping techniques.

Developing the ability to tolerate distress entails learning to avoid situations of extreme discomfort until you are ready to cope with them.

Some examples of distress tolerance practices taught in dialectical behavior therapy include taking a cold shower or exercising vigorously to help one feel more grounded.

You can learn to bear distress by practicing radical acceptance, another technique from dialectical behavior therapy.

When you practice radical acceptance, you can learn to accept the things you can't alter, including your ideas, feelings, and circumstances.

This dialectical behavior therapy ability requires awareness and deliberate action toward accepting reality as it is, flaws and all. To accept something as it is for the sake of moving on is the essence of radical acceptance; it does not imply approval of the circumstance.

Management of emotions

Rather than allowing your emotions to dictate your behavior, the fourth basic skill of dialectical behavior therapy (DBT) is emotional regulation.

The ability to control one's emotions requires:

- Verifying one's reality
- Embracing one's feelings
- and mastering the inverse of the acts linked to particular feelings

For example, when engaging in opposite actions, you disregard your emotions and act in a contrary manner.

If you're feeling particularly low and critical of yourself, for instance, it could be a sign of your emotions to retreat to a dark room and lie down. The polar opposite of staying indoors would be to go outside and enjoy the sun as it sets.

You can keep your emotions in check by engaging in opposite action. Actually, what you're doing is learning to tune into your emotions ("I know how I feel") and then deliberately acting in a way that changes your trajectory.

Some Cases of Dialectical Behavior Therapy for Adolescents

It is still very new that DBT has been formally adapted for use with teenagers. Hence, particular adjustments for teenagers with certain diagnoses or needs are still the subject of ongoing research. Some programs may be implementing changes that lack research backing.

However, the discipline is still in its infancy, so the programs that are experimenting with changes are the trailblazers—and they could potentially achieve remarkable outcomes. Inquiring about a program's outcome data is always an option if you have concerns. Some of the following diagnoses and conditions have shown encouraging results with DBT modifications in research.

Drug-Free Treatment for Adolescents Suffering from Depression, Anxiety, and Thoughts of Self-Injury

Much of what we've covered thus far originates from dialectical behavior therapy (DBT)-A program that aims to help people who are depressed, anxious, suicidal, or have thoughts of self-harm, Lowered motivation, disinterest in activities, worse grades, disturbed social interactions, hazardous behavior, self-harm, suicidal ideation or behavior, and diminished social support are common symptoms among adolescents coping with these challenges. Ensuring safety is the top priority for programs at all times. After resolving any obstacles to therapy, the next step is to enhance quality of life and acquire new skills.

As a result of the DBT, the typical duration of a program is sixteen weeks. Nevertheless, a graduate group is available for an additional 16 weeks to review and solidify abilities. The severity of symptoms before starting therapy determines whether the duration of these groups is enough to stop treatment altogether.

Therapy may need to continue after an adolescent has finished if the severity of their problems was severe to begin with or if there were obstacles to therapy. Your area may provide different programs, or you may want to return to standard outpatient therapy as part of your recovery plan.

Dialectical Behavior Therapy for bipolar illness

Adolescents who have bipolar disorder may benefit from dialectical behavior therapy (DBT). The procedure utilized with the teenagers was mostly unchanged from the standard DBT-A program, with just minor modifications made.

Adding a section on psychoeducation about bipolar illness and dialectical behavior therapy (DBT) was the primary program change. Three aspects of emotional vulnerability were also brought to light by the researchers: the responsiveness, the strength, and the length of time that affective responses last.

Afterward, therapists could associate particular emotional states with corresponding skill sets and desired outcomes. The focus was on helping the teens recognize their emotions and choose the right skills to deal with them. In addition to DBT, the youths also received psychopharmacology therapies under supervision.

A two-pronged approach was developed for the treatment of bipolar disorder in teenagers. There were six-month segments to the program. Over the first half of the year, patients attended 12 sessions of individual therapy and six sessions of family therapy on a weekly basis. With just six sessions of each, that number is halved during the maintenance phase of therapy, the second part of the program. As is customary, the therapist advised the client on whether to continue therapy or end treatment when the course was complete.

Talk Therapy for Eating Disorders

There is limited evidence that dialectical behavior therapy (DBT) can help individuals overcome their eating issues. Adolescent DBT treatment for eating disorders is an emerging field with promising early results. The Canadian day treatment program served as the setting for Pennell's research.

Cultural pressures on body image provide an invalidating environment that needs to be properly addressed in the treatment of eating disorders. We updated the diary cards so that they now also track food consumption and behaviors relevant to eating disorders in addition to symptoms and goals. There was a heavy focus on caregiver assistance, as in past teen versions.

Family-Based Therapy and Dialectical Behavior Therapy were part of this program. A minimum six-week commitment and parental support were both required by this program. Program length and components for dialectical behavior therapy (DBT) for eating disorders can vary greatly depending on the program's focus.

Can Teens Rely on Dialectical Behavior Therapy?

Adaptations of dialectical behavior therapy (DBT) for adolescents are a recent development. Still, studies conducted so far have consistently demonstrated beneficial results. Miller and Rathmus, who created DBT-A, were trailblazers in studying dialectical behavior therapy (DBT) with teenagers. The DBT-A adaption has Marsha Linehan's stamp of approval.

DBT for teens continues to have favorable outcomes, according to meta-analysis reviews and other research. One or two. Multiple settings, including residential treatment, inpatient treatment, juvenile detention, and others, have shown success with dialectical behavior therapy (DBT).

New adaptations will be developed, and existing ones will have their knowledge base expanded through ongoing research. When it comes to pushing for more study, the Linehan Institute is unrivaled. On top of that, fresh research about DBT is consistently being produced by a large number of colleges both in the US and abroad.

Among the many abilities that make up Emotion Regulation, "Opposite Action" stands out. Teens with mental health concerns, such as anxiety, low self-esteem, trauma, anger control, and depression, can benefit from this skill. A quick rundown of the operation of this DBT skill is what we'll provide here.

When Should You Oppose Your Action?

When your current painful emotion isn't appropriate for the circumstance or isn't helping you cope, use Opposite Action. As an example, imagine a teen who experiences intense feelings of humiliation whenever she enters a classroom. She has no reason to be embarrassed because she did nothing wrong in the eyes of her classmates or instructors. Nevertheless, she consistently experiences feelings of guilt, worthlessness, and low self-esteem each time she enters that class. Therefore, she rarely raises her hand or speaks out in class.

Opposite Action is a useful tool right now.

Instead of acting on her emotion—shame—which is unproductive and out of touch with reality, she should do the exact opposite. Returning to her chair, she wishes she could hide, be unobtrusive, and keep quiet. Her instructions from Opposite Action are to enter the room with a straight back, stand tall at her desk, and push up her chest. Keeping her hand up and responding to questions is what Opposite Action says she should do. Despite how challenging it will be for her, I still say yes.

An Overview of DBT's Opposite Action

It is the central tenet of Dialectical Behavior Therapy that altering one's behavior, even inadvertently, causes one's emotions to shift. Similarly, if a depressed adolescent wants to lie in bed all day, they should do the complete reverse. They need to get ready and leave the house immediately. Even if they first resist getting out of bed, dialectical behavior therapy (DBT) suggests that they will feel better if they do so. Even though a depressed adolescent may believe they don't have or deserve to feel better, Opposite Action encourages them to force themselves to engage in pleasurable things that they once enjoyed, such as cooking, painting, athletics, reading, or anything else.

Things to Avoid When Using Opposite Action

It is not recommended to apply all skills simultaneously in DBT. In some situations, Opposite Action is not the best move to make. You shouldn't utilize the Opposite Action when your reaction is completely warranted and fits the facts of your scenario.

Imagine a teen who is embarrassed or guilty about cheating on a test the day before and is now facing the consequences of having their papers returned to them in class. Guilt is a completely reasonable emotion to feel here. Feelings of shame and remorse are understandable for this adolescent. In this case, the inverse course of action—doing nothing to feel guilty, being self-assured, and standing tall and proud—would not be appropriate. The adolescent would instead be asked to think of ways to address the issue of dishonesty. It could be helpful if they approached the teacher after class to clarify the situation. Another option is to consult their parents for guidance.

I'll give you one additional example. The adolescent is nervous about making it home alone at two in the morning. There are a couple of masked men coming up behind you in the pitch blackness of the night. Feeling anxious is a reasonable response in this case. A state of anxiety would be appropriate in this situation. Consequently, the adolescent should give in to the want to flee and hide. Opposite Action, which would entail confidently and calmly approaching the other figures, walking up to them, and talking with them, is probably not a smart choice due to safety concerns.

Various DBT Skills for Adolescents and Their Benefits

Treatment for adolescents focuses on teaching them Opposite Action and a number of other dialectical behavior therapy techniques.

Teens can practice mindfulness, a form of dialectical behavior therapy (DBT), to help them focus on the here and now rather than fixating on the past or worrying about the future.

One of the dialectical behavior therapy (DBT) tasks for teens is interpersonal effectiveness, which teaches them to stand up for themselves while also realizing that they won't always be right. Another skill that DBT teaches is emotional regulation, which is all about understanding other people's emotions without passing judgment. Adopting this ability enables teenagers to develop into adults who are emotionally stable and caring.

Tolerance for emotional distress: Adolescents can learn to control their emotions with the help of dialectical behavior therapy (DBT) techniques.

Practice Dialectical Behavior Therapy Skills at Home for Teens

Instruction in dialectical behavior therapy (DBT) methods that teens can practice at home supplement what they learn in therapy. To name a few examples:

- "Go with the Flow": a technique for enhancing skills in dialectical behavior therapy (DBT) for managing emotions

- Moreover, rather than but: Reducing the usage of the word "but" teaches kids that their viewpoint isn't the only one that matters.

- Keep the Past in the Past: This skill practice teaches teens that it's harmful to dwell on the past.

The individual needs of each teen patient and the treatment approaches used in the dialectical behavior therapy adolescent program will determine the specific "homework" instructions for DBT skills.

Ability to cope with and overcome strong emotional experiences

Sometime in our lives, we all face a crisis. Divorce, death, or job loss are all examples of major life events that might trigger such crises. These crises can be little, like being stuck in traffic, having to wait in line at the checkout, or just being at a loss for what to dress. In order to survive a crisis, it is helpful to develop DBT distress tolerance abilities.

TIPP, ACCEPT, improve, make a pros and cons list, self-soothe, and radical acceptance are all part of the process.

TIPP

You've hit a wall emotionally. Perhaps this is the worst that can happen, or perhaps it was merely the "last straw." Your DBT toolbox should include the TIPP distress tolerance skill. This ability will help you descend off the precipice, figuratively speaking (I hope not literally).

Timed breathing, temperature, intense exercise, and paired muscle relaxation make up TIPP.

The weather

Our bodies tend to feel hot when we're angry. In response, you can either hold an ice cube in your hand, spray your face with cold water, or turn on the air conditioning in your automobile. Reducing your core temperature can help you feel better on all levels.

Strenuous Workout

Exercising vigorously will amplify your strong emotions. Do you not run marathons? It's all right; being isn't necessary. Exert yourself to exhaustion by running to the end of the street, swimming laps, or jumping jacks. Lowering stress levels is facilitated by increasing oxygen flow. Furthermore, when you're tired, it's hard to maintain a dangerously angry demeanor.

Respiratory Rates

A simple practice like breathing exercises can have a significant effect in alleviating emotional distress. Breathing exercises come in a variety of forms. Exhale your favorite if you have one. A method known as "box breathing" can be used in such a situation. There will be a four-second pause between each breath. Breathe in for four seconds, hold for four more, exhale for four more, and hold for four more. And the process begins anew. Remain in this breathing rhythm until you experience a sense of calmness. Keeping your breath steady lowers the stress hormone cortisol.

Relaxing Your Muscles Together

Partial muscle relaxation is an intriguing scientific field. A voluntary muscle will remain more relaxed after being tense, relaxed, and then allowed to rest than it was before tense. When you let your muscles relax, you need less oxygen, which means your heart rate and breathing rate will decrease.

Focusing on a specific set of muscles, like your arms, is one way to give this method a go. Constrict your muscles to their maximum extent for five seconds. Subsequently, release the stress. When you give your muscles a break, you'll feel yourself letting go, too.

ACCEPTS

The DBT acronym for distress tolerance. The ability to bear unpleasant emotions until you can deal with and overcome them is a key component of the ACCEPTS framework. The 90s comedy Friends features Monica dating Pete Becker in the show's first season. He tells her, "We need to talk," over the phone while he's out of town. To Monica, the question of whether it is a good or bad chat looms large. As she waits for his return, she is experiencing psychological distress. While she waits for Pete to return home, she utilizes her skill set known as ACCEPTS.

Tasks, Contributions, Comparisons, Emotions, Distancing, Thoughts, and Sensations make up this dialectical behavior therapy skill. Until you can figure out how to fix the issue, these methods will help you control your emotions.

Things to do

Get moving, and it can be anything that helps you stay healthy. Do some reading, whip up some strawberry jam, take a stroll, give a pal a call, or perhaps even do the dishes. Doing something that occupies your time and distracts you from the negative feelings will assist. When you've finished, it's time to switch things around. (While you wait for that dreaded situation, you may have a really productive day!)

Contributing

Act kindly toward another individual. There are two ways in which helping others can alleviate mental suffering. As indicated before, performing an act of service might sometimes serve as a distraction from the current issue. Furthermore, helping other people makes us feel good about ourselves, which can be a stress reliever in and of itself—assisted with household chores, such as preparing dinner, mowing the grass, or making cookies for someone special. You can take your mind off of the problem at hand by considering any of these contributing ideas.

Comparisons

View your life through a different lens. Can you think of a period when you had it worse than you have right now? This might be the most intense circumstance and feeling you've ever felt; however, it's also possible that it's not. (In that case, you might have to return to the TIPP part.) Is anyone else out there who has gone through more pain than you have? Are you safe in your own home while people in another region of the globe scramble to find what they need following a natural disaster? The point of this practice is not to make things worse for you emotionally and psychologically. Use this skill instead to see your current situation via a new lens.

The Feelings

You can choose to feel the complete opposite of whatever you're feeling right now. Just fifteen minutes of meditation can help calm your racing thoughts. Do a Google Image search for "cute puppies" if you're in a bad mood. (A Google search for "ugly puppies" should provide the humor you're seeking.) To lessen the impact of a negative feeling, it is helpful to provide a dose of the opposing emotion.

Remove Distractions

Ignoring an issue for a while is acceptable when you aren't ready to face it head-on. One strategy for avoiding is practicing mindfulness or diverting one's attention to something else. You have the option to schedule a future visit to address the matter. It will be taken care of, so you may relax for now.

Thoughts

Try repeating the letters of the alphabet backward or solving a Sudoku puzzle to divert your attention away from worried, negative thoughts. Meanwhile, while you work on controlling your emotions, these diversions can help you refrain from damaging behaviors.

Sensation

When you're upset, try to calm yourself by using all five senses. Soaking in a hot bath with a lavender bath bomb and some calming music, munching on a familiar snack, or settling in to watch a favorite show are all examples of self-soothing behaviors. A sensory experience can help you deal with the here and now.

Things that are accepted, things that are contributed to, things that are compared, feelings, thoughts, and sensations.

Tolerating your discomfort until it's time to settle the situation is one of the ACCEPTS dialectical behavior therapy skills. Other abilities, like dialectical behavior therapy (DBT) interpersonal effectiveness, might assist you in meeting your requirements after you are prepared to confront the issue directly.

Make things better

In many cases, you will feel helpless in the face of an unsavory occurrence, regardless of how minor (you just shattered your shoe) or major (you just shattered your foot). To get through these tough moments without resorting to unhealthy habits, you require distress tolerance. Strong feelings pass quickly. Dialectical behavior skills IMPROVE can help you deal with intense emotions till they pass.

Aim for the present moment, imagine a meaningful experience, pray for guidance, relax, take a vacation, and be encouraged.

Imagery

Visualize yourself resolving the issue at hand, maintaining your composure, and then experiencing a sense of fulfillment once it is over. Doing so could potentially alter the problem's resolution in your favor) Significance

Look for the silver lining amid the darkest times. Is there anything valuable you've taken away from this? Perhaps you will develop greater empathy. Perhaps you will form new connections. Perhaps this will set you on the path to recovery. Think of a cause—or at least a plausible one—to explain your current hardship.

The offering

Whatever helps you most is the best way to pray. God or the cosmos are just two examples of possible higher powers to whom one can pray. Give up trying to fix things and beg for a little more time to be patient.

Relaxation

The "fight or flight" response causes us to stiffen up whenever we're under pressure. To alleviate the mental anguish you're feeling, partake in activities that bring you relaxation. A calming stroll, yoga, a hot bath, or deep breathing are all examples of what may be considered these hobbies.

Just one item right now

Forget about the past and plan for the future; just be here. No amount of bringing up previous problems or worrying about what might happen in the future will help resolve the current issue. Zero in on a single activity and give it your undivided attention. Keeping one's thoughts focused makes it easier to manage intense emotions.

Time off

In a perfect world, when you get back from your vacation, you're recharged and ready to tackle whatever problems awaited you when you got back. In the midst of a crisis, few of us can afford to take a true vacation. You could instead go on an imaginary getaway. Picture yourself in a different place, perhaps enjoying a sunset walk around the lake or cruising along the PCH. Feel free to extend your "vacation" for as long as you need to and come back whenever you need to. I hope that when you "return," you will be better equipped to handle your current situation.

Positive reinforcement

A third party is unnecessary for encouragement to have any impact. Recite meaningful statements to yourself, like "I got this," "I can improve this moment," or "¡sí se puede!" to motivate yourself. Raise your voice and be proud of it! When faced with adversity, you will be astounded by your capacity to inspire yourself to persevere.

A better life through imagery, meaning, prayer, relaxation, focusing on the here and now, taking a vacation, and receiving encouragement.

When faced with an unchangeable issue, you can always turn to the distress tolerance tactics outlined in IMPROVE. If you use these methods on little difficulties, you'll find that they're second nature when the big ones come.

CHAPTER 5

ADVANCED STRATEGIES FOR PERSONAL GROWTH

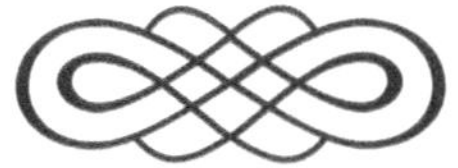

Even though development and fixed mindsets have a lot of support in the fields of psychology and education, you won't hear much about them in casual conversation.

How Can Teens Benefit from a Growth Mindset?

Being a teenager is a time of developing a growth mindset, which is the belief that one's intelligence and abilities may be enhanced via hard work and the application of effective tactics. Adolescents who have a growth mindset are able to reflect on and improve upon their past failures and failures in school and in life. They consider setbacks to be stepping stones on the road to success and perceive difficulties as learning experiences.

People who have a growth mentality know that intelligence and natural ability are only the starting points. They have the insight to know that skills may be developed with time and effort. This mindset cultivates an insatiable curiosity for knowledge and the tenacity to accomplish remarkable feats.

Instead of fixating on their flaws, adolescents with a growth mindset look at what they're capable of accomplishing. This mode of thinking is based on the belief that one's present self does not necessarily reflect one's eternal self.

Explain What a Fixed Mindset Is to Adolescents.

Adolescents who hold a fixed mindset consider their IQ and other abilities to be static characteristics, similar to skin tone or eye color. Adolescents with a fixed attitude are less likely to succeed academically because they are impatient and seek easy ways out of problems. Because they don't yet have the mentality to bounce back from failure, young adults let this thinking make failure feel insurmountable.

Adolescents with a fixed perspective think that natural ability is the only key to success. At any cost, they get fixated on being intelligent or talented. Instead of trying and failing, individuals learn to stay away from tasks where they have a low chance of success. Adolescents should not adopt this mentality.

Some teenagers may hold a fixed mindset perspective, which holds that one's IQ and other personality attributes are static characteristics that cannot be changed.

Appearing intelligent and covering up apparent flaws is, in their view, the only way to achieve success. Something that can happen to teenagers is that they start to limit themselves and define themselves by the things they think they can't achieve.

The integration of CBT and DBT

When you're a teenager, you're dealing with a lot of feelings, new situations, and obstacles. The strength of all-encompassing coping mechanisms becomes apparent when life feels like a roller coaster. Come with me as I investigate how a hybrid approach combining CBT and DBT can be your best weapon in overcoming life's challenges.

Grasping Your Mental Self: Using CBT Together

Talk therapy is like having a mental toolbox full of superhero powers. It's about being aware of and combating those deceptive thoughts that can influence your emotions. Envision yourself with a miraculous mirror that magnifies your ideas. You can learn to recognize when your ideas are causing you distress with cognitive behavioral therapy.

So, what's the deal with this enchanted mirror? Think of it this way: You face a difficult circumstance, such as an exam or a quarrel with a buddy. Asking oneself, "Are my thoughts helping or hurting me?" is a skill taught in cognitive behavioral therapy. You can improve your mood and resilience by becoming aware of negative ideas and then challenging them to become constructive and good ones.

Embracing Harmony: The Journey with DBT

Using DBT, let's add some excitement now. Take a role-playing journey where you're trying to learn how to embrace change and acceptance. As you navigate emotional awareness and self-acceptance, DBT's mindfulness practices will serve as your reliable guide.

The practice of mindfulness is like taking a miraculous potion: it keeps you fully immersed in the here and now. You learn distress tolerance in dialectical behavior therapy (DBT), which equips you to confront difficulties directly, even while you're feeling extremely emotional. Having this barrier around you will keep you safe in dangerous situations.

"The Dynamic Duo: CBT + DBT"

Combining dialectical behavior therapy (DBT) and cognitive behavioral therapy (CBT) creates a powerful coping mechanism. Think of CBT as the planning stage of a video game and DBT as the exciting adventure. Cognitive Behavioral Therapy (CBT) assists in making plans by analyzing thoughts. In contrast, dialectical behavior therapy (DBT) teaches you to confront problems directly.

When you're worried about a large project, cognitive behavioral therapy (CBT) might help you identify negative ideas like "I can't do this." Mindfulness practices are incorporated into dialectical behavior therapy (DBT) to help you remain calm and focused after challenging unpleasant thoughts. It would be the same as having a strategy and being able to carry it out perfectly.

A Customized Program for Your Mental Health: Your Journey

It is essential for teens pursuing mental well-being to establish their own unique regimen. Create a program that works for you by combining CBT and DBT techniques. A strong formula for stability and resilience might be your daily habit, whether it's writing in a notebook, practicing mindfulness, or doing what you love.

With the support of cognitive behavioral therapy and dialectical behavior analysis, you can become the protagonist of your own narrative. Adopt an adventurous spirit, confront obstacles head-on, and cultivate a robust mindset; they will serve as compass points as you navigate the thrilling path of adolescence.

Customizing Care to Meet Each Patient's Unique Requirements

It is critical to think about the client's unique requirements and objectives when deciding whether CBT or DBT is more suited for them. People suffering from extreme emotional instability or interpersonal problems may benefit more from dialectical behavior therapy (DBT), which takes a more holistic approach and focuses on emotion regulation, than from cognitive behavioral therapy (CBT), which is more structured and problem-focused and hence better suited to those seeking short-term treatment for conditions like anxiety or depression.

Can CBT and DBT be Adapted?

Because of their flexibility, cognitive behavioral therapies like CBT and DBT can be modified to meet the specific requirements of each patient. Based on the client's requirements and treatment objectives, therapists may combine aspects of both methods. For an anxious patient, a therapist may recommend cognitive behavioral therapy (CBT) and dialectical behavior therapy (DBT) mindfulness practices. Because of this flexibility, individualized treatment programs can be created to increase the likelihood of successful outcomes.

Deciding on a Counselor

Make sure the therapist you choose has experience and training in cognitive behavioral therapy (CBT) or dialectical behavior therapy (DBT) before you commit to their services. The client's comfort level with the therapist is crucial in establishing a strong therapeutic bond, which in turn improves therapy outcomes. It is important for clients to feel comfortable asking prospective therapists questions about their background, training, and treatment philosophy to make sure they are qualified to meet their unique requirements.

CHAPTER 6

JOURNAL PROMPTS FOR THE PRACTICE OF EMPOWERMENT

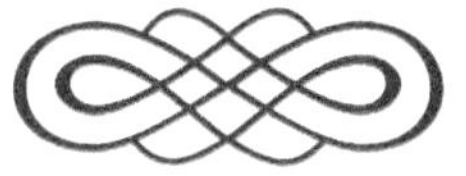

People of all ages can benefit greatly from keeping a journal. Furthermore, as adolescent knowledge is always evolving, it might be an ideal opportunity to discover more about oneself and the world.

We have compiled 99 motivational journal prompts that are ideal for teenagers to help you overcome those "aaargh!" moments when you don't know what to write or have any ideas. I guarantee that you will reach for a pen and paper as soon as you see these prompts!

Journaling for what reasons?

For those of you who are still on the fence about keeping going after the thoughts stop flowing, let's take a brief look at the advantages of journaling before we get into it.

The main advantages of maintaining a diary include the following:

- It's safe to write in a journal since no one will judge you. Whether it's a huge or little memory, write it down and let it all hang out. No need to worry about what others think!

- If you're having trouble processing some emotions or thoughts, keeping a journal can be a great place to write them down.

- It has a lot of healing and relieving effects. I had a day that was difficult or unclear? Explaining what happened and how you felt about it in writing will help you understand the situation better.

- We promise to keep your information private for as long as you require it.

Keeping a journal has many benefits, including:

- Expanding your understanding of yourself and your aspirations

- Establishing a habit of writing for enjoyment that will last a lifetime

- Learning to take it easy, pay attention to your surroundings, and think about what's truly important to you

- Developing a growth mindset through journaling

- Having the tools of self-awareness and creativity to navigate the challenges of adolescence

The benefits of using journal prompts

"I long to put pen to paper, but my true desire is to unleash the multitudes of emotions that are concealed within my soul."

Anne Frank's Diary

But what can you do when you find yourself at a loss for words to describe how you really feel? What if you don't think your thoughts are interesting enough to put on paper? Maybe you're simply not thinking about anything important.

There you have it! Journal prompts are perfect for that!

Teens benefit greatly from journal prompts because:

- They motivate you to start and maintain a regular journaling habit

- They reveal hidden thoughts and ideas

- They inspire you to write about a wide range of interesting subjects, from weighty social justice issues to silly "what if" questions!

- They are made to make you think and feel, which is a great way to learn more about who you are

- Avoid using complicated arguments or studies! Anything goes; there's no pressure to make it perfect.

Here are some ideas for teenage diaries, so read on! It's entertaining, serious, creative, and thought-provoking all at once.

High school, friends, family, social media, and the future are some of the personal topics covered. Many others look at society as a whole or at hypothetical events. Rest assured, there is an option for every individual!

Furthermore, we have included additional questions and suggestions for each prompt to ensure that you have much to consider in the event that these suggestions do not stimulate your imagination sufficiently.

Adolescents' mindful journaling prompts

For all the right reasons, mindfulness is all the rage these days.

One of the most useful study skills for improving grades is learning to pay attention in the here and now and complete tasks at hand. On top of that, it's fantastic for the state of mind.

So, to get you started on the path to mindfulness, here are some excellent reflection and grounding prompts.

1. How are you feeling at the exact moment?

Stop for a moment. Take note of the physical sensations, the spectrum of emotions you're experiencing, and any remaining concerns or fears you may have. Make a note of them.

2. On a daily basis, how do you make time to relax and recharge?

What are your current activities? How can one remove pessimism from their thoughts? How crucial is it for you to pause and enjoy that tranquil moment? Document this practice.

3. Where do you feel most at peace?

Tell me about your favorite spot for relaxation, the one you go to when you can't sleep. Why is this place so special to you?

4. To whom do you express your gratitude?

What do you appreciate most about the individuals who love you when you consider their presence in your life? Things you've done together, moments you've spent together...? Take pleasure in the range of feelings it evokes.

5. What are you most prone to putting off until later, and why?

Could you please tell me any responsibilities in your life and academics that you tend to put off till later? At this very time, how can you give your whole attention to these duties?

Being a procrastinator is normal, whether you're a teen or an adult. Use this journal prompt to get better at managing your time and getting things done!

6. Provide an account of how you begin your day

What are your responsibilities? In the mornings, how does your routine set the tone for your day? Is it hectic, energized, concentrated, or calm?

7. Describe someone whose perspective has shifted from your own.

The adage "Don't judge a book by its cover" is well-known. Describe an experience in your life where you felt this way.

Maybe there was someone whose present and past you failed to fully comprehend before passing judgment on them. Are these still people you know?

8. Tell me about the moment this week when you felt the most relaxed.

Think back on a time last week when you were completely relaxed and at ease. Put it in writing!

Encouragement to write in a journal about typical adolescent experiences

Your life as a teenager is likely hectic, complicated, and full of things you don't give much thought to on a daily basis.

Use one of these prompts to jot down some cherished and long-forgotten memories from your adolescent years. In addition, you'll find them really interesting to read in your later years!

9. What activities do you enjoy doing with your friends?

Is staying home more your style? Where are you most often seen? Is there a particular café or study place that you like? When you're both here, how does life normally go?

10. Having a best buddy is a great asset. Depict them in writing!

Why are they important to you? Your friendship blossomed; how did it begin? Tell me what you make of their friendship.

Describe the characteristics of an ideal friend if you do not currently have one.

11. In what ways do you think video games have shaped your character?

Can you say that video games are fun for you? Describe the life lessons you've gleaned from playing video games if that's the case. To what extent have they influenced your identity and aspirations?

12. How has the rise of social media impacted your daily life?

Include details about the people you've met, the things you've done, and your daily social media interactions in your piece. What emotions does it evoke in you? Do you long for the admiration it bestows? How has it affected those in your immediate vicinity?

13. Is there a difference between your online and offline behavior?

Describe the many relationships and experiences you've had in writing. Which of your personas do you identify with more, and why?

14. What is your go-to dish?

Do you know who makes the best version? It brings back what kinds of memories? On what regular basis do you get to indulge in it?

15. Dedicate a piece to your beloved location.

Give me some details about your favorite spot. Feelings that it brings up? Go there with who? Is there a specific place you'd rather be by yourself? Is it a frequent stop for you?

16. What would be your ideal weekend activity?

When you have it off, who or what do you hang out with? Are you more of an adventurer, a homebody, or a social butterfly?

17. Have you ever considered how your hometown may have shaped your character?

How exactly? Do you take pride in the impact your hometown has made on your life?

18. In your parents' eyes, what is the most significant duty they have entrusted to you?

Think about everything from housework to babysitting that your parents have requested of you. Does it bring you joy? How has it impacted you as a developing teenager?

19. What does your reflection seem like the first thing in the morning before school?

Upon first reflection, what is your self-perception? Before anything else, do you find fault with how you look? If so, why? Do you have any self-loving qualities that you appreciate when you wake up?

Or are you already preoccupied with academic matters...

20. Make a piece of writing that reflects your strongest beliefs.

What is the source of your belief? Who or what had an impact on it? To you, what does it mean to be a strong advocate for your beliefs?

21. What changes have you experienced in the past several months?

Tell me how you feel about them. How are you handling them? Jot down how these developments have impacted your life and ideas, regardless of your opinion on the matter.

Reflecting on the past and strengthening your memory through journaling

Now that you're a few years older, you should have plenty of wonderful memories from your childhood that you'd like to hold on to.

However, we are fallible; we often fail to recall the little pleasures that life has to offer.

Here are some excellent ideas for teen memory journal prompts: Their effectiveness is doubled! In addition to keeping a record of special experiences, they will strengthen your memory for all the schoolwork that teenagers have to do.

22. Today, what new information did you acquire?

Jot down a brief synopsis of everything you learned in class today, including the main ideas, formulas, and principles covered.

What you picked up today doesn't have to be dry and theoretical; perhaps you discovered some interesting trivia or gained some insight into the lives of those close to you.

23. Think back on a good thing that happened this week.

I want to know what happened to make you so joyful. Tell me who you were nice to. Are you aware of somebody who showed you kindness?

24. Describe an experience this week when you were happy with yourself.

Why were you so happy and fulfilled? Was it a calm or a tumultuous moment? So, who else was in your party?

25. Tell me about the most difficult thing that happened to you this week.

When you reflect on this challenge, what accomplishments can you take pride in? Regrets? If so, what are they? If yes, then explain your reasoning and tell me how you'll tackle your next obstacle.

26. Describe an instance when you were just too embarrassed to cry.

What made you laugh? Are you tempted to chuckle again just thinking about it? Did the people around you share your amusement?

27. How does your life's narrative contain any surprises?

Try to put yourself in the shoes of someone staring at a mosaic of their life's moments. The shards range in size from quite large to quite small. How do they convey the story? Is the significance of any of the parts something you were not expecting?

28. Can you think of a time when you went above and beyond for another person?

How did you react to it? What emotions did it evoke in them? Would you do it all over again? How proud are you of what you did?

29. Tell the story of a time when you were at your most vulnerable.

If you had opted for a different path, how would things have turned out differently now? If you could travel in time with your parallel self, where would you go?

(I know it's not easy, but writing in a private notebook is the ideal way to unleash pent-up emotions when you face challenging questions and events.)

30. Describe an experience when you overcame a fear and attempted something new.

What transpired? Who enticed you to do it? How did you react to it? When you think back on this experience, what feelings come to mind?

31. Do you have a favorite memory from your childhood?

You love it, but why? How often are anecdotes about this event in the family?

Also, here are some fantastic substitutes: Can you share a hilarious memory from your childhood? May I ask you about your first memory?

32. Recount the most memorable part of your summer trip

Tell me about your favorite part of that summer trip: the people, the location, or the things you did there. Is it possible for you to make it again?

33. What was your go-to plaything when you were a kid?

Are there any memorable moments from your time together? Do you recall the reasoning for your selection, and what is their name?

34. Were you a kid who had an imaginary friend?

If yes, then document them! Could you tell me who they were and how they behaved? Describe the experiences you shared.

Encouragement for teens' personal growth through journaling

You don't have to dwell on the past or the present to benefit from journaling. Additionally, it can be a wonderful method to investigate your future aspirations. There must be plenty for an adolescent like you; opportunities are just beginning to present themselves.

Make use of these diary prompts to ponder the many paths your life could take as you navigate adolescence and beyond!

35. In the coming year, what routines do you hope to alter or establish?

Jot down a realistic strategy after giving serious consideration to the actions that would be required to bring this to fruition.

36. Describe a major decision you'll soon have to make.

What options are available to you? How different would your life be in ten years if you followed each of these paths?

Put yourself in the role of valedictorian and picture yourself delivering the commencement address. Do you have any advice for your fellow students or advice you would give to your younger self? Who will you celebrate with, and what will you do first after the ceremony?

37. Compile a list of all your lifelong goals, whether large or small. This list will serve as a "bucket list."

Who or what will you prioritize, and how will you get things done? Collect some entertaining things and begin...

Is there anything on your list that seems really far away? Create a strategy to turn them into attainable long-term objectives.

38. In your opinion, what is one area where you feel you might use some further knowledge or insight?

Choose a topic that piques your interest—be it a societal concern, a fascinating area of study, or a practical use of what you've learned in the classroom. I need your help figuring out how to study this.

39. For what do you hope history will remember you?

Describe the kind of impact you hope to have on the world; there are many avenues open to you. Abilities, successes, acts of kindness, loved ones...

40. Right now, tell me the kind of work that would fit you the best.

Think about how tomorrow you'd like to apply for a summer job in order to put some money toward your college expenses. Could you tell me your strengths? Could you use some training in a certain area? Which career path would put your abilities to the greatest use?

41. Express your motivations in writing.

Exactly what is it that drives you? In the past, how has this inspiration helped you stay motivated and achieve your objectives?

Why not write about what you find out about methods to increase your motivation if you're not feeling motivated? There are plenty available!

42. when you think about being older, what do you most anticipate?

What part of childhood do you long for the most? Write down all the good and bad things about being a teenager using this diary prompt.

43. What would you do for a living if you could do anything?

In your opinion, what is the most extreme response that comes to mind? Despite the fact that it may not be feasible in the modern world, what specific passions do you have that you would want to turn into a profession?

44. Compose an autobiography

Give an account of your current day, including your feelings, concerns, hopes, and dreams. Give it your all so it captures who you were as a teenager.

It will be ready to open in five or ten years, so put it somewhere secure.

45. What would you like to ask your former self?

What are your hopes and fears for the future, and for yourself in particular? In the years to come, who will be your closest pals, and how will you spend your free time? Feel free to inquire about anything that piques your interest!

As a wonderful journaling exercise for your future self, put them in a secure place and return to them in five years to read and respond.

Teens' mental health: journaling prompts

Journaling is a wonderful tool for mental health; it helps you work through intense feelings and thoughts until you can collect yourself and decide what to do next. Also, no one will judge you (and you should hope that no one judges you, too!).

Take advantage of these journaling prompts to help your troubled adolescent overcome their anxiety, fears, and excessive worries. Believe me, it'll be beneficial.

46. What concerns are you clinging to at the moment?

Are your concerns from the past weighing you down today? Describe them in detail, leaving no stone unturned. Think about how it would feel if you could release those concerns.

47. Is there anything out of the ordinary that is terrifying you at the moment?

Do you ever find yourself fretting over the worst-case scenario? Make one of these scary situations more bearable by writing about it. Create a plan of action for when these possibilities really materialize!

48. In your piece number forty-eight, describe a bad memory that has stuck with you.

Do you find it difficult to get past unpleasant, humiliating, or embarrassing memories? Stop them in their tracks by putting pen to paper and sharing how that experience has shaped you.

Was it productive in any way? Has your self-awareness expanded? Try to see the bright side and detach yourself from the memories.

49. When you're feeling worried, upset, or depressed, what physical sign do you notice first?

Are you able to consistently recognize when it's occurring? In order to alleviate these emotions, what steps can you take?

50. When you think about anything, what does it make you nervous?

To distract yourself, jot down three things. Just write down three realistic things you can do; maybe even journaling about it would help!

51. Which subjects do you find difficult to broach?

Do you know the reason? Could you speak to someone else instead? If that doesn't work, try the time-honored "Dear Diary" method and write in your journal.

52. Make a note of all the things that annoy and upset you

You can control some of these things, but others are beyond your sphere of influence. Is there anything you can do to make this list shorter?

Alternatively, make a note of all the things that are bringing you joy at the moment; of these, how many are within your sphere of influence?

53. Which colors would you use to paint your current mood, and why?

What associations do you have with the colors? How many are required? Do you see a realistic or abstract painting?

Teen Identity Exploration Journal prompts

Teenage years are filled with ups and downs as you figure out and rediscover who you are.

If you're looking for some teenage-related introspection and contemplation, these diary prompts could be perfect for you!

54. What changes have you made compared to last year?

How does looking back at your history make you feel? Has your body gone through a lot of changes in the last year? Have you rearranged your priorities?

55. If you were to characterize yourself, how would you say it?

Everyone, from your parents and friends to your instructors and even complete strangers, is an important person in your life. How would they describe you, and are you OK with their selections?

Why not consult some pals if you're still unsure? Discovering your own unique set of traits can be a breeze with this prompt as a jumping-off point.

56. What are the things that make you happy?

In what ways do you find humor? How often do you decompress?

57. Who are you while you're in public?

How much of who you are do you prefer to keep under wraps? Why? Does it seem like someone is trying to hide your true self from you, and what are your options for addressing this?

58. What sets you apart from the rest?

Are there any peculiarities about your personality or hobbies? Do you possess any unique abilities?

59. In your opinion, what are your strongest character traits?

Explain in writing which ones are the finest and why. What additional features would you like to create, and what steps can you take to begin?

60. In your life, who have you looked up to the most?

Which of their traits do you find most admirable? Does anyone you know know them, or are they famous? How does that impact your perception of their character? What makes them special in your eyes?

61. In your life, who can you rely on the most?

Can you tell me why that is? By your estimation, which of your acquaintances has the greatest faith in you? Do they have any inside information about you?

62. when you look in the mirror, what do you see?

Any success, no matter how big or tiny, should be documented. Whether it's in the realm of academia, charity, or social activism, what have you accomplished that you are most proud of? Tell me what you think.

63. What are your favorite things to do?

What are some ways that you may include these into your regular routine? What is it about them that makes you happy?

64. Express in writing the burden of your own unreasonable expectations.

Is it your culture, your friends, or your parents from whom they originate? In what ways do you strive to meet their expectations? On occasion, do you decide to go off on your own?

65. What is your idea of an ideal situation?

Why (or why not) do you aim for it? Is your happiness, mental health, and overall quality of life affected by your pursuit of perfection?

66. Jot down everything that motivates you in this world.

Pay attention to the details. Before expanding your thoughts to the entire globe, consider your immediate surroundings and the people in it.

67. When someone compliments you, how does it make you feel?

How are you feeling right now? Take the compliments or leave them? How does it make you feel when someone criticizes you?

68. Are you more comfortable being an observer or a participant?

Can you explain your emotions? What life events have influenced this response? Do you ever deviate from the rule?

69. Have you ever found yourself in a very challenging conversation? Put it in writing!

Just what was the topic? So, how did you deal with it? How would you approach this discussion differently if you were to have it all over again?

70. If you had children, what would you never do differently than what your parents do now?

Why? What life events have influenced this response? Do you see them as positive or negative?

71. Give a description of five things that exemplify who you are.

Describe them. These things were your choices, but why? Would you say they're items you love doing or wearing?

72. have you ever parted with a valuable possession?

For what reason and to whom did you gift it? How did you react to it? Is it something you'd revisit?

Journaling ideas for teenagers with a global conscience

Much reflection on our personal and communal life is required in light of the current uncertain circumstances.

Any problem, no matter how big or little, may be improved with your aid; use these diary prompts to think about it! Consider political stances, environmental issues, social enterprises, etc.

Regardless of your age, these diary prompts might serve as a starting point for contemplation of the many things that are on your mind.

73. If you could change the world for just one other person, what would it be?

By helping, whom would you choose to make a difference? What makes them special? If you were in charge, what would you do to make their lives better?

74. What's one easy thing you could do differently right now?

Can you think of even one little action you could do every day to make a difference in the world? Is it possible for you to regularly do it?

From gardening to yarn bombing to litter picking, no notion is out there!

75. How do you think bias has impacted your life and the community around you?

Describe in writing an instance of injustice that you have experienced. Do you feel it aimed at you or at those around you?

Defeating these biases would have what kind of impact on your daily life?

76. What rules are most difficult for you to comprehend in your life?

Write down the reasons you don't want to follow a rule you'd like to see changed.

Whether at home, in the classroom, or in society at large, how would you go about your day if you battled to have this rule changed? If you could alter this rule, how would things change? Not only in theory but in practice, too?

77. Compile a list of all the things you hate and want to rebel against.

Discuss any topic you like, no matter how big or tiny! You chose these concerns, but why? Do you have the guts and resources to face any of these (with friends)?

78. In today's world, what is something that scares you?

Actually, what are some things you could do to alter that? Then, picture yourself taking action to alter that situation if you possessed the means to devise and fund a remedy.

79. Express your thoughts on a city or town that may use some TLC.

Can you think of a way to change it? What are your options? Are you able to determine what materials would be required to carry it out? Give a description of the area once you've accomplished it and the emotions you'd experience.

80. Which three aspects of the world would you alter and explain your reasoning behind the changes you would make?

Explain in writing the global impact of the three items you've selected. Do they have any merit? Would there really be an improvement?

81. how can you make a positive impact in your neighborhood this year?

Choose anything—large or little—and put your thoughts on paper. Could you possibly pull it off? How much would it cost? Would you get any support from your friends or school to reach your objective?

82. Does your community place a high enough priority on individual privacy, in your opinion?

How has that changed your life? Would you like more personal space? In what ways does the influence of your peers influence how you manage your online persona and data?

83. What would you study if you had the chance to become an expert in anything?

Imagine yourself ten years from now, well-educated and ready to dominate your industry. As an expert, how would you go about making a difference in the world?

Engaging and imaginative teen journaling prompts

The opportunity to answer all the ridiculous hypotheticals is one of my favorite kinds of journaling prompts.

If you're having trouble relating to the weighty concerns posed above, try writing about your adolescent experiences with one of these lighthearted prompts instead. Maybe next year, you'll have a different takeaway!

84. Paint a picture of yourself exploring your favorite work of art.

How did you find yourself inside of it? What would it be like to exist in two dimensions? Describe the world as it would appear.

85. Envision yourself five inches taller when you awaken tomorrow...

In what ways might that alter your view of yourself? Consider the implications for your daily existence. Would some concerns go away while others would stay?

86. What would you do if someone gave you $5,000 but said you couldn't spend it on yourself?

In what ways might you put it to use, and why? Is it more important to you to share the wealth among many people or to lavish it on one? Who would you prioritize: acquaintances or total strangers?

87. Picture your life on screen and propose it!

Can you think of a title? To Hollywood, what story would you propose for this film? The craft that proposal! In your opinion, who should play the main roles?

88. What would constitute beauty if every individual on this planet had a uniform appearance?

Would it continue to play a significant role in society? Is the term "beautiful" even appropriate? If we had to pick one quality that defines beauty on Earth, what would it be?

89. Imagine for a second if you could transform into a character from your beloved comic book or graphic novel.

Would you rather play the part of the hero, the sidekick, the villain, or an innocent bystander? If you could change the plot in any way, how would you do it?

90. Which imaginary universe would you choose if you could live there?

Why? Would you rather be yourself or pretend to be a certain character? Do you think you could alter the plot somehow?

91. To which fictitious figure do you feel the closest affinity?

Where do you find their qualities most admirable? Give some examples of how the things you have in common shape your identities.

92. Set a scene where you go through time to see your family's ancestral home.

What would you ask a long-lost relative if you had the chance to spend a day in their shoes? How would their daily routine look?

93. You get to pick the year of your life you replay. Put it in writing!

Tell me which year you'd choose and why. Would you change a thing, or is there a specific event you wish you could relive?

94. Picture yourself confined to an elevator with three complete strangers.

Did you consider approaching them? Just what would you like to discuss? In a perfect world, who would you most like to be shackled to?

What if someone had just given you an old recreational vehicle (RV) to transform into a private, intimate hanging spot for you and your pals?

95. Describe the ideal gathering place.

Tell me how you would make it your ideal living quarters. What materials would be required? Would you take it somewhere specific?

96. Tell me about the house of your dreams.

Imagine it for a second. In that case, who would you choose to live with you? In this situation, what is your age?

97. Tell me which animal you'd most like to spend a day as if it were your own identity and why.

What characteristics and freedoms does the creature possess? For what reasons do you see yourself reflected in them?

98. On a desert island, what would you bring with you? 98.

What made you decide on them? For what reason are they useful to you? Is their purpose functional, amusing, sentimental, or?

99. Tell me about the new technology you've invented.

Just what is it? Does the technology you need perform a single function? Alternatively, is its utility more generalized? If it were useful on any planet, what kind would it be?

CHAPTER 7

THE PRACTICE OF EMPOWERMENT: EXERCISES

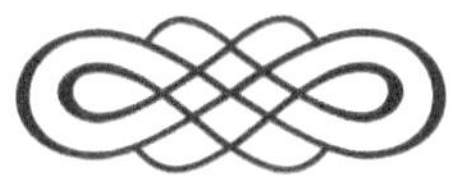

ere are exercises tailored for teens to practice Cognitive Behavioral Therapy (CBT) and Dialectical Behavior Therapy (DBT) skills:

1. Thought Record Journaling (CBT):

- Grab a journal and create columns for "Event/Thought," "Emotion," "Evidence For," and "Evidence Against."

- When faced with a challenging situation, write down your thoughts, associated emotions, evidence supporting those thoughts, and evidence contradicting them.

- Analyze and challenge any distorted thoughts, replacing them with more balanced alternatives.

2. Mindful Breathing (DBT - Mindfulness):

- Find a quiet space and sit comfortably.

- Focus on your breath, inhaling and exhaling slowly.

- Pay attention to the sensation of breath entering and leaving your body.

- If your mind starts to wander, gently bring it back to your breath.

- Practice this for 5-10 minutes daily to enhance emotional awareness and reduce stress.

3. ABC PLEASE (DBT - Distress Tolerance):

A: Accumulate Positive Emotions:

- Engage in activities that bring joy or relaxation. It could be reading, listening to music, or spending time with loved ones.

B: Build Mastery:

- Set a small goal or learn a new skill. Achieving these small victories boosts confidence.

C: Cope Ahead:

- Anticipate challenging situations and plan coping strategies in advance.

PLEASE: Take care of your Physical Health:

- Attend to your basic needs - eat well, get enough sleep, and exercise regularly.

4. Challenging Core Beliefs (CBT):

- Identify a negative core belief you may have about yourself (e.g., "I'm not good enough").

- Collect evidence from your experiences that contradict this belief.

- Write a positive affirmation based on the evidence gathered.

- Repeat the affirmation regularly to challenge and reframe the negative belief.

5. Values Exploration (DBT):

- Identify your core values - qualities and principles that are important to you.

- Reflect on how well your actions align with these values.

- Set small, achievable goals that align with your values.

- Regularly assess your actions and adjust them to stay true to your values.

6. Gratitude Journaling (CBT):

- Create a gratitude journal.

- Each day, write down three things you're grateful for.

- Reflect on the positive aspects of your day, fostering a more optimistic mindset.

7. Opposite Action (DBT - Emotion Regulation):

- Identify an emotion you're experiencing, such as sadness or anger.

- Choose an action opposite to what the emotion is urging you to do.

- For example, if you're feeling sad, engage in an activity that usually brings joy or connect with a friend.

8. Cognitive Restructuring with Images (CBT):

- Identify a negative thought you often have about yourself.

- Create a mental image that represents this thought.

- Gradually transform the image into a more positive or neutral one.

- This exercise helps reframe negative self-perceptions.

9. Radical Acceptance (DBT):

- Identify a situation causing distress.

- Practice radical acceptance by acknowledging the reality of the situation without judgment.

- Repeat a mantra like "It is what it is," emphasizing acceptance of the present moment.

10. Behavioral Activation (CBT):

- Identify activities you used to enjoy but have stopped doing.

- Create a schedule incorporating these activities into your routine.

- Notice the impact on your mood as you reintroduce positive and fulfilling activities.

11. Daily Mood Tracking (CBT):

- Create a simple mood tracker in your journal or on your phone.

- Rate your mood at different times throughout the day.

♦ Identify patterns and triggers, helping you become more aware of your emotional fluctuations.

12. TIP Skills for Distress Tolerance (DBT):

T: Temperature Change

♦ Splash your face with cold water or hold an ice pack to your eyes for a quick mood boost.

I: Intense Exercise

♦ Engage in brief, intense physical activity to release pent-up energy and tension.

P: Paced Breathing

♦ Practice slow and controlled breathing to calm your nervous system.

13. Behavioral Experiments (CBT):

♦ Identify a belief you want to challenge (e.g., "I can't make new friends").

♦ Conduct small experiments to test this belief, such as initiating a conversation with a classmate.

♦ Observe the outcomes and use them to challenge and reshape your beliefs.

14. Non-Judgmental Mindfulness (DBT):

♦ Practice mindfulness without judgment.

♦ Observe your thoughts and feelings without labeling them as good or bad.

◆ This helps foster a more accepting and non-reactive mindset.

15. Graded Exposure (CBT):

◆ Identify a situation or activity that causes anxiety or discomfort.

◆ Break it down into smaller, manageable steps.

◆ Gradually expose yourself to each step, building tolerance and reducing anxiety over time.

16. Self-Compassion Break (CBT):

◆ When facing a challenge or mistake, practice self-compassion.

◆ Acknowledge your struggle, remind yourself that it's a shared human experience, and offer kind words to yourself.

17. PLEASE MASTER (DBT):

Prioritize taking care of your Physical Health.

◆ P: Physical Illness

◆ L: Balanced Eating

◆ E: Avoiding Mood-Altering Substances

◆ A: Balanced Sleep

◆ S: Exercise Regularly

- Paying attention to these aspects can positively impact your overall well-being.

18. Automatic Thought Monitoring (CBT):

- Throughout the day, become aware of automatic negative thoughts.

- Use a small notebook or an app to jot down these thoughts.

- Challenge and reframe them with more balanced or positive alternatives.

19. DEAR MAN (DBT - Interpersonal Effectiveness):

When advocating for your needs or setting boundaries, follow the DEAR MAN framework.

- D: Describe the situation
- E: Express your feelings
- A: Assert your needs
- R: Reinforce positive behavior
- M: Stay Mindful
- A: Appear confident
- N: Negotiate if needed

20. Visualization for Goal Setting (CBT):

- Visualize yourself successfully achieving a goal.

- Break the goal into smaller steps and vividly imagine each step.

- This exercise helps enhance motivation and focus on achieving objectives.

21. Radical Mindfulness (DBT):

- Practice mindfulness by fully engaging in an activity, such as eating a meal or taking a walk.

- Focus your attention on the sensory experiences, like taste, smell, or touch, to anchor yourself in the present moment.

22. Three-Column Technique (CBT):

Use a three-column table to identify and challenge negative thoughts.

- Column 1: Write down the negative thought

- Column 2: Identify the cognitive distortions in the thought

- Column 3: Develop a more balanced or positive thought

23. Building Mastery through Hobbies (DBT):

- Choose a hobby or skill you'd like to develop.

- Set achievable goals, practice regularly, and track your progress.

- This not only builds mastery but also serves as a healthy distraction.

24. Future Pacing (CBT):

- Imagine a positive future scenario in detail, such as succeeding in a goal or overcoming a challenge.
- Focus on the emotions, sights, and sounds of that imagined success.
- This exercise can boost motivation and create a positive mindset.

25. PLEASE YOURSELF (DBT):

Similar to PLEASE MASTER, but focusing on personal well-being.

- P: Physical Health
- L: Balanced Eating
- E: Avoid Mood-Altering Substances
- A: Get Adequate Sleep
- S: Engage in activities that bring you joy

26. Mindful Coloring (DBT - Mindfulness):

- Engage in coloring as a mindful activity.
- Focus on the colors, the sensation of the crayon or pencil, and the movement of your hand.
- This can serve as a calming and centering practice.

27. Double Standard Technique (CBT):

- Apply a double standard to your negative self-talk.

- If you wouldn't say it to a friend, challenge and reframe the thought as you would for a friend.

- Foster self-compassion and kindness towards yourself.

28. DEARMAN GIVE (DBT - Interpersonal Effectiveness):

Use the DEARMAN framework with an additional focus on being gentle, interested, Valid, and Easy-mannered.

- G: Be Gentle in your approach

- I: Be Interested in others

- V: Validate their feelings

- E: Use an Easy manner during communication

29. Socratic Questioning (CBT):

When faced with a challenging thought, ask yourself Socratic questions to explore its validity.

- What's the evidence for and against this thought?

- Are there alternative ways to view this situation?

- What would I tell a friend who had a similar thought?

30. ABC PLEASE MASTER in Daily Routine (DBT):

Incorporate the principles of PLEASE MASTER into your daily routine.

- P: Physical Health
- L: Balanced Eating
- E: Avoid Mood-Altering Substances
- A: Get Adequate Sleep
- S: Engage in activities that bring you joy

31. Cognitive Restructuring Through Art (CBT):

- Express your thoughts and emotions through art.
- Create a visual representation of a challenging thought or emotion, then modify it to reflect a more positive perspective.
- This exercise combines artistic expression with cognitive restructuring.

32. ACCEPTS (DBT - Distress Tolerance):

Practice ACCEPTS when facing distress.

- A: Activities - Engage in a distracting activity.
- C: Contributing - Do something nice for someone else.
- C: Comparisons - Compare yourself to others in a less fortunate situation.
- E: Emotions - Intense exercise to release emotions.

- P: Pushing Away - Mentally put the issue aside for a while.

- T: Thoughts - Change your thoughts by focusing on something else.

- S: Sensations - Engage in a physical sensation to distract from emotional pain.

33. Positive Affirmations (CBT):

- Create a list of positive affirmations that challenge negative self-talk.

- Repeat these affirmations daily, especially during challenging moments.

- Encourage the development of a more positive self-perception.

34. Nonviolent Communication (DBT - Interpersonal Effectiveness):

Apply nonviolent communication principles in your interactions.

- Observe: State the observable facts.

- Feelings: Express how you feel.

- Needs: Identify your needs in the situation.

- Requests: Make clear requests for what you need.

35. Behavioral Rehearsal (CBT):

- Practice behavioral rehearsal before facing a challenging situation.

- Envision yourself successfully navigating the situation, anticipating positive outcomes.

- This mental rehearsal enhances preparedness and confidence.

36. Observing Your Thoughts (DBT - Mindfulness):

- Take a few minutes to sit quietly and observe your thoughts.

- Practice non-judgmental awareness, letting thoughts come and go without attaching to them.

- This exercise helps you develop a mindful approach to your thinking patterns.

37. Cost-Benefit Analysis (CBT):

- When faced with a decision or dilemma, conduct a cost-benefit analysis.

- List the perceived costs and benefits of different options to help make informed choices.

- Consider short-term and long-term consequences.

38. Building Mastery in Social Situations (DBT):

- Choose a social situation that feels challenging.

- Set a small goal to navigate that situation comfortably.

◆ Gradually expose yourself to more complex social interactions, building social mastery.

39. Positive Visualization (CBT):

◆ Visualize a positive future scenario in detail, imagining success and achievement.

◆ Engage all your senses and emotions to make the visualization vivid and motivating.

◆ This exercise enhances a positive mindset and goal-oriented thinking.

40. Mindful Walking (DBT - Mindfulness):

◆ Take a mindful walk, paying attention to each step and your surroundings.

◆ Focus on the sensations of walking, the sounds, and the rhythm of your breath.

◆ This exercise promotes mindfulness and helps ground you in the present moment.

41. Values Clarification (CBT):

◆ Identify your core values and beliefs.

◆ Reflect on how your actions align with these values.

◆ Set specific, value-driven goals to guide your decisions and behavior.

42. Half-Smile Technique (DBT - Mindfulness):

- When faced with stress or tension, practice the half-smile technique.
- Gently curve your lips into a half-smile, even if it feels forced.
- Notice how this physical change can influence your mood and reduce stress.

43. 100% Attention (CBT):

- Engage in a conversation or activity with 100% attention.
- Put away distractions and focus entirely on the present moment.
- This exercise enhances connection and active listening skills.

44. Self-Validation Journaling (DBT):

- Acknowledge and validate your own feelings in a journal.
- Write down your emotions, recognizing that they are valid, regardless of external opinions.
- Practice self-compassion and acceptance.

45. Automatic Thought Redirection (CBT):

- When you catch a negative thought, intentionally redirect it to a positive or neutral alternative.
- Create a mental cue or phrase to signal the redirection.

♦ This exercise helps reshape automatic negative thinking patterns.

46. Mindful Listening (DBT - Interpersonal Effectiveness):

♦ Practice mindful listening during conversations.

♦ Give your full attention, avoid interrupting, and show genuine interest in what the other person is saying.

♦ This exercise enhances communication skills and builds connections.

47. Decatastrophizing (CBT):

♦ Identify a situation causing anxiety.

♦ Challenge catastrophic thoughts by considering more realistic and less extreme outcomes.

♦ This exercise helps manage anxiety by reframing catastrophic thinking.

48. Radical Openness (DBT - Interpersonal Effectiveness):

♦ Practice being radically open in your communication.

♦ Share your thoughts and feelings honestly, even if they feel vulnerable.

♦ This fosters authenticity in relationships and reduces emotional suppression.

49. Behavioral Chain Analysis (DBT):

- Analyze a challenging situation by breaking it down into smaller parts.

- Identify the chain of events, thoughts, and emotions leading to the outcome.

- This exercise helps gain insights into patterns and triggers.

50. Positive Self-Talk Mirror Exercise (CBT):

- Stand in front of a mirror and practice positive self-talk.

- Compliment yourself, acknowledge achievements, and challenge any negative thoughts.

- This exercise promotes self-compassion and boosts self-esteem.

Feel free to explore and experiment with these exercises, incorporating them into your routine as needed. Each exercise contributes to building valuable skills for emotional well-being and personal development.

Tips for creating a personalized mental wellness routine

1. Make time for yourself. Almost every method of self-care begins with this fundamental requirement. It needs to be a regular part of your schedule and take time. With everything else going on, it can be not easy to carve out time for yourself, but doing so is essential. It will become second nature if you begin immediately. A lot of the things

listed below won't use up much of your time; in fact, some of them will only take about fifteen or twenty minutes. Consistency is what matters.

2. Mindfulness training. Since meditation was seen as hocus pocus, we have made great strides. In addition to being an excellent tool for alleviating stress, anxiety, and depression, research has shown that practicing mindful meditation can alter brain structure and function. There are a lot of resources available online, such as instructive videos on YouTube or apps for smartphones, or you can consult an expert in person. You can do this whenever you need to, wherever you are!

3. The practice of yoga. Stretching, increasing flexibility, and establishing a connection between mind and body are all aspects of Eastern exercise practices like yoga that have long been practiced for their stress-relieving and health-promoting benefits. You can learn Yoga from videos online, but going to a studio is the best option.

4. Get some moving. Exercising can be done in various ways. Aerobic exercise, strength training, and endurance training are all available. You may get a lot of exercise and fresh air just by walking two miles every day. Exercising regularly not only makes you fit, but it also has natural antidepressant and antianxiety effects.

5. Turn in for the night. Getting enough sleep is essential for a healthy mind, body, and spirit; nevertheless, it is easier said than done. If they want to perform at their peak, most young people require a good night's sleep, preferably eight or nine hours. There's a lot of academic, social, and

recreational commitment, so squeezing this in isn't simple, but the reward is worth it. Your "biological clock" will likely remember when it's time to sleep and wake up if you maintain a regular sleep schedule.

6. They are expressing one's creativity. Pick an artistic medium that allows you to express yourself freely. Keeping a journal, composing poetry, painting, drawing, taking photographs, dancing, or playing an instrument all fall under this category. The trick is to find a creative outlet for your feelings. Some people take painting seriously and enroll in classes. Still, there are plenty of talented people who learned their craft on their own and managed to pull it off. Also, don't be too hard on yourself! Dispelling negative emotions and thoughts is as easy as losing oneself in creative pursuits.

7. Have fun taking care of a pet. Having a pet may be one of the best methods to encourage self-care if you're fortunate enough to have one. Understand what I'm getting at if you own one. Having a pet as a constant companion, caring for them, and experiencing their affection unconditionally is a rare occurrence.

8. Get together and talk to your pals. Meeting with peers and discussing personal issues, particularly those from the past that you are still processing, can help avoid burnout and improve overall health, according to research. Social interactions are crucial for the release of feel-good neurotransmitters and the development of resilience. Also, only chatting isn't required for the tasks. Activities such as making art, playing with slime, or gaming (Dungeons & Dragons is incredibly popular again!). Every

day. Having a small number of truly meaningful friends can have a profound impact on your life, regardless of how many "friends" or "followers" you may have.

9. Take time to enjoy Nature. Our beaches, rivers, and parks—both public and private—are highly valued for good reason. Consider the last time you went on a beautiful hike, rode your bike through a park, played in the snow, or even just strolled around your neighborhood, all while enjoying a breathtaking dawn or sunset. Do you feel that way again? Suppose we can take a few moments away from our phones and the hustle and bustle of everyday life. In that case, we can reconnect with nature and experience the joy it brings.

10. Put down your phone (for a few hours). Working on it is challenging. Contrary to popular belief, you are not required to wear it at all times. Even if it's only for a few hours, you can take a break. If you're feeling anxious or withdrawing because you can't be there for something you perceive as crucial, take a moment to reflect. Do you require instantaneous access to a certain number of SMS, Instagram stories, or other forms of digital communication? Scarcely any? Taking a break from the continual notifications could really be rather pleasant once you give it a go.

11. Act selflessly and help a stranger. Humans are hardwired to help others. Giving actually makes us feel better than receiving things because of the endorphins our brains release. There is no better way to feel good about yourself than to become involved in community service, even if it's only a little bit. Volunteering at places like soup kitchens,

elderly living centers, children's hospitals, or after-school programs is a great way to meet new people and make a difference.

CHAPTER 8

Towards a Resilient Future: Setting Goals and Moving Forward

Teens have lofty aspirations and ideas, but they lack the expertise to plan and execute a strategy effectively to achieve their goals. Aims like "Save enough money for a car" or "Get an A+ in all of my classes" are set to fail or be disregarded.

Without proper preparation, setting a goal could have the opposite effect of encouraging a growth attitude. The adolescent may reflect on the setback by saying, "See? In any case, I'm not up to the challenge.

Comprehending and establishing one's own objectives

With the right amount of planning, persistence, and good fortune, setting and achieving goals can be a source of great satisfaction and fulfillment.

Young people must learn the skill of goal setting. Remember that it's difficult to go anywhere without first deciding where you're going. Teens who set goals for themselves are better able to concentrate on the steps necessary to reach those goals, which in turn helps them to be more efficient with their time and resources and to recognize when they may need assistance.

What are the Benefits of Teens Having Objectives?

Accomplishing the intended outcome (the pinnacle of every goal!) is only one of many advantages that teens can reap from mastering the art of goal setting.

- gaining self-assurance as they go along;
- learning to work hard and become more efficient;
- figuring out what drives them;
- becoming more resilient in the face of setbacks;
- knowing when to seek assistance and when to accept it

Teens are better able to put their ideas into action when they set goals. Individually, academically, and professionally, these abilities will be invaluable to them.

Adolescence is a wonderful time of life, full of hope and possibility. But aspirations are insufficient for material prosperity. To make your aspirations a reality, you must first set goals. By establishing sensible objectives, you can pave the way to realizing your aspirations. This article will discuss ten wise objectives that teens might establish to achieve their aspirations.

Prompt Academic Performance

Achieving academic success is fundamental to developing one's potential and opening doors to new opportunities. The information, abilities, and opportunities available to you are greatly influenced by your level of education. You can get closer to your college hopes and aspirations if you commit to doing well in school.

Take stock of your current academic situation and make note of any areas that could use some work. Improve your study habits, become an active participant in class discussions, and get better marks in difficult classes by setting specific academic goals. To stay focused and keep track of progress, break down these goals into smaller, more doable activities.

Achieving academic achievement requires the development of efficient study methods. Determine how you learn best and commit to a regular study schedule that works for you. Establish consistent study times, make your study area peaceful and well-organized, and make use of study tools like textbooks, websites, and study groups. Put in the time, but don't forget to use effective tactics like noting and summarizing problem-solving practice and frequent review.

Furthermore, look for ways to expand your mind outside of the confines of academia. Make plans to join clubs or competitions that interest you, do independent research, or study things that fascinate you. Participating in extracurricular activities related to your major shows that you are passionate about and committed to your chosen field of study, which will serve you well in your future academic endeavors.

Maintaining a healthy work-life balance is essential if you want to achieve academically. Take care of yourself first, keep your relationships strong, and find ways to spend your free time that make you happy. Academic success is considerably more than just getting good marks; it's also about developing a lifelong curiosity for knowledge and a strong work ethic.

Growth on an Individual Level.

Putting money into self-improvement is like embarking on a life-altering quest; it will lead you to your dreams and help you reach your full potential. Establishing objectives for one's own development is crucial for boosting self-assurance, refining one's abilities, and fostering one's interests.

You should begin by thinking about what parts of self-improvement speak to you. Make it a point to read literature that will challenge your assumptions and deepen your understanding. Developing your critical thinking and empathy abilities, reading broadens your horizons to include many cultures, ideas, and experiences.

Also, make it a point to do things that interest you, like learning something new or taking up a hobby. Activities that need regular practice, such as learning an instrument, programming, painting, or playing a sport, can help you develop self-control, imagination, and expression.

One of the most important parts of growing up is learning to believe in yourself. Intentionally challenge yourself by setting goals to do things that are out of your comfort zone. Some examples of this would be taking part in leadership opportunities, becoming a member of a debate club, or practicing public speaking.

Take setbacks in stride and use them to become a stronger, more resilient person. Get yourself in the company of upbeat people and look for ways to improve your life by learning from those who have already succeeded.

Improving one's communication abilities is also an important part of self-improvement. Aim to become a better communicator in writing, as well as in speaking and listening. Suppose you want to become a better communicator. In that case, you should participate in writing contests, attend public speaking classes, or start a school newspaper. Personal and professional relationships can flourish when people are able to express themselves clearly and concisely.

Establishing objectives in the realm of personal development will pave the way for an ongoing process of self-improvement and growth. Recognize your progress, take stock of your accomplishments, and be flexible with your life objectives as you change. Your success, fulfillment, and joy are investments in yourself that you can make through personal development.

A Balanced Way of Life

Teens should make it a priority to live a healthy lifestyle since it improves overall health and lays the groundwork for a happy and prosperous adulthood. Making a plan to take care of yourself physically and mentally can give you the stamina, concentration, and determination to go for your aspirations.

Get in the habit of exercising regularly by establishing a goal for yourself. Get some exercise most days of the week for at least half an hour. Whether it's swimming, dancing, running, or playing a sport, find something you want to do. Exercising on a regular basis has several health benefits, including better physical fitness, improved happiness, less stress, and better cognitive performance.

A healthy diet should be one of your primary objectives, along with regular exercise. Make it a point to eat a wide variety of fruits and vegetables along with complete grains, lean meats, and healthy fats. Refrain from eating or drinking too many processed foods, sugary snacks, or sodas.

Establish concrete objectives, including increasing water consumption, preparing healthful meals at home, and bringing packed lunches to work. Incorporating even little, long-term adjustments into your diet can have a huge effect on your health.

Maintaining a healthy mental state is just as critical. Motivate yourself to do things that help you relax and unwind, like meditation or deep breathing exercises, so you can better manage your stress.

Taking care of yourself should be a top priority, so make sure you get adequate sleep, practice mindfulness, and reach out to people you trust for assistance. Always keep in mind that taking care of your physical, mental, and emotional health is an integral part of leading a healthy lifestyle.

Investing in yourself by committing to a healthy lifestyle can provide you the stamina and excitement to chase your dreams. To lay the groundwork for a full and balanced life, embrace the power of self-care routines, healthy diet, and regular exercise. If you want to succeed in life, you need to take care of your health, which is your most valuable asset.

Taking Charge of One's Money

As a teenager, you can make good financial decisions and lay the groundwork for a prosperous future by learning to be responsible with your money. Achieving success in managing your finances depends on your ability to set and achieve goals in this area.

The first step is to decide how much of your income you want to put away. Set aside a certain percentage or amount each pay period to go toward savings, whether it's from a side hustle, an allowance, part-time employment, or some other source.

The discipline and financial security that come from starting this practice at a young age are priceless. First things first: open a bank account or savings account. That will make things much easier. Divide your savings between short-term targets, like buying that thing you want, and long-term ones, like paying for education or investing.

A budget should be established and adhered to, in addition to savings goals. Keep tabs on your earnings and outgoings to see exactly where your money is going. Divide the budget into sections for necessities like food, transportation, and school costs and for wants like entertainment and new clothes. Knowing that you have the funds to cover all of your necessary purchases can alleviate any concerns you may have.

In order to make wise financial decisions, it is important to differentiate between needs and wants. Make it a point to cut back on wasteful spending and look for ways to save money, such as looking for sales, comparing costs, or trying new, less expensive options. By following these steps, you can avoid seeking financial assistance that could lead to unsettling obligations.

Additionally, make it a priority to educate yourself on the fundamentals of personal finance. Learn all you can about investing, credit, and interest rates. Research personal finance by reading up on the subject or enrolling in a course online.

You can better manage your credit, save for the future, and borrow money if you have a firm grasp of these ideas. You can gain financial independence and important life skills like responsibility, work ethic, and time management by seeking opportunities to earn money through side hustles or full-time jobs.

Benefit to Society

Finding meaning and fulfillment in life can be as simple as setting a goal to positively impact the world and your community. Becoming more empathetic, more capable as a leader, and more invested in the welfare of others are all outcomes of intentionally working toward social impact objectives.

Aiming to volunteer for a worthy cause should be your first step. Look for neighborhood groups or organizations that deal with issues close to your heart. Decide how many hours a month you want to spend volunteering, or list everything you want to do.

Volunteering has several benefits, including helping people in need, expanding your horizons, and strengthening your capacity for empathy and compassion.

Aim to plan community events or projects in addition to your volunteer work. Find a social issue that truly moves you, and then figure out how you can help bring attention to it and make a difference. You have the power to affect your community and take action on significant issues, whether you organize a charity fundraising, start a community clean-up campaign, or start a project led by youngsters. Leadership is crucial in sports. Therefore, you may even coach a team. Regarding this, adopt a development attitude because taking small steps can lead to bigger ones, allowing you to make an even bigger impact in your social circle.

Also, make it a priority to get to the community leader position. For example, you may join a student government, a club, or an organization with a mission to improve the world; you could also improve your leadership abilities by learning to work better with others and solve problems creatively. Be a role model for others to follow and encourage them to participate in social impact projects. Inspiring and rallying people around a shared cause is a hallmark of effective leadership.

Always keep in mind that even the smallest, most mundane activities can have a profound effect on society. Aiming for a positive social influence means you want to make a difference in the world. Volunteer, organize, lead, and ultimately, be the change you want to see. If we work together, we can make our society kinder and more welcoming to everybody.

Discovering Your Ideal Professional Path

Suppose you want to find your calling and build a successful career. In that case, one of the first steps is investigating various employment options. The best way to learn about your options, make educated choices, and lay the groundwork for your future success is to establish objectives while you explore potential careers.

Start by deciding what hands-on experience you want in different areas that interest you. If you are interested in a certain field, look for ways to shadow people who work there. This will give you a good idea of what it's like to work in various fields daily and what kind of education and experience are necessary for each.

You should also consider making it a priority to intern or join an apprenticeship program. Through these programs, you can learn by doing, obtain valuable experience, and expand your professional network.

In addition, make it a point to attend workshops, career fairs, and networking events. You may network with experts worldwide, learn about exciting new career opportunities, and get sound advice at these events.

Make it a point to learn as much as you can about the various fields and the skills they demand. You can consult experts, read books, and peruse online resources to increase your knowledge and get insight into your interests.

Aim to acquire academic credentials and work experience and Emphasize the development of abilities related to communication, problem-solving, collaboration, and flexibility. Because these abilities can lead to better jobs and more money, it's a good idea to participate in extracurricular activities, join groups, or take on leadership responsibilities that provide them opportunities to hone.

Discovering your ideal job is an ongoing process that changes as you do. Set goals to investigate multiple career paths and enjoy discovering who you are. In searching for a career that matches your abilities and interests, be receptive to new chances, look for a mentor, and be flexible. In addition to helping you attain your financial goals as a teenager, creating objectives for career exploration can put you up for a prosperous and satisfying professional future.

Internet Duty

To protect yourself and your reputation in today's digital world, you must act responsibly when using the internet. Establishing objectives for digital responsibility can help you stay secure while online, safeguard your personal information, and utilize technology with care.

First things first: make a plan to keep your digital footprint positive. Make it a point to consider the consequences of your internet actions before publishing them. Think about the people who could see the photos, comments, and information you post online and the impact that could have.

Try to maintain an upbeat and courteous online persona representing who you are and what you stand for. In addition, make it a point to use social media with care. Establish limits on your time on social media and stick to them. Use social media to broaden your horizons, gain knowledge, and spread important messages.

In addition, make plans to safeguard your personal information when you're online. Go through all your internet accounts, including social media, and make sure your privacy settings are up to date. Get into the habit of making strong, one-of-a-kind passwords for all your accounts.

Make it a priority to educate yourself about online threats and best practices for protecting your digital identity. Exercise caution when providing personal information online and stay vigilant against any phishing or scam attempts. You may avoid danger and have a more secure time online if you take measures to protect your privacy.

Goals for improving one's capacity for critical thinking when engaging with digital media should also be considered. It is crucial to differentiate trustworthy sources from those that spread false information or misinformation due to the abundance of online information. Determine that you will check the information before passing it on and challenge the sources' reliability. To verify the accuracy of the material, look for trustworthy websites and fact-checking groups.

Keep in mind that being a responsible and conscientious online citizen is what digital responsibility is all about. By establishing objectives in this domain, you solemnly vow to make ethical and empowering use of technology. Make the most of the internet while being wary of its dangers.

Do your best to safeguard your privacy, be well-informed online, and have a positive digital influence. You may use technology to your advantage while keeping a healthy distance from the internet if you prioritize digital responsibility.

Efficiently Utilizing Time

Achieving your goals, making the most of each day, and striking a good work-life balance all depend on your ability to manage your time wisely. You may enhance your productivity, stay organized, accomplish your goals, and prioritize work by setting goals for time management.

Make it a priority to create a schedule you can stick to daily. Find the sweet spot for studying, finishing homework, participating in extracurriculars, and unwinding. To make sure you receive adequate sleep, establish regular wake-up and bedtime routines. Establishing regular patterns in your day can help you feel more secure, reduce decision fatigue, and give your whole attention to the things that matter.

Also, make it a point to work on your ability to plan ahead and prioritize tasks. Determine in advance what you need to accomplish so that you may make a list or use an app to help you keep organized. Assign reasonable due dates and divide big jobs into smaller, more manageable chunks. Determine which tasks are most pressing and important, then give your full attention to those. Minimizing procrastination and ensuring each work gets enough time can be achieved by creating goals to plan and prioritize efficiently.

In addition, make it a point to plan ways to maximize your efficiency and reduce interruptions. Determine what is getting in the way of your productivity, whether it's social media, too many notifications, or bad habits, and plan to fix it.

You can disable notifications while concentrating on a certain task or schedule when you can check social media. Establishing a suitable, distraction-free space to study or work should be one of your objectives. You may increase the quality of your work and your ability to concentrate by making it a mission to work in an area free of distractions.

You can't get back the time you've already spent on something important. You may improve your productivity and health by committing to and sticking to a schedule. Planning, prioritizing, and minimizing distractions can have a profound impact. More time for what matters most—pursuing your hobbies and enjoying leisure activities—less stress and more productivity—all results from practicing disciplined time management. Aiming for this is a wise move.

Being Culturally Aware

In today's globally interdependent society, it is crucial to cultivate cultural awareness to inspire compassion, tolerance, and insight into the experiences and viewpoints of others. Aiming to increase one's cultural awareness is a great way to meet individuals from many walks of life, learn about new perspectives, and dispel prejudice.

Make it a priority to learn about other cultures. Learn about different cultures by reading about them or watching documentaries online.

Make it a priority to educate yourself about cultures distinct from your own, whether they are far away or close by. Talk to people from different cultures and try to put yourself in their shoes to learn about their customs, beliefs, and experiences. One way to broaden one's horizons and develop openness and curiosity is to make it a personal mission to learn about other cultures.

More than that, I resolve to actively participate in cultural events and gatherings. Come celebrate many cultures at community events, exhibitions, or festivals. Indulge in the rich variety of cuisine, music, art, and traditions. You can improve your own social influence and that of teens by acquiring this knowledge and then passing it on to them.

Intentionally seek opportunities to talk to people from other cultural backgrounds and share your experiences and perspectives. Participating in cultural activities is one way to help build a more accepting and diverse society. This will help you understand other cultures better and broaden your perspective.

Aim Establishment and Self-Reflection

To keep yourself motivated, record your progress, and make any required revisions along the way, goal setting and reflection are potent activities. Achieving your hopes and ambitions requires setting goals and reflecting on them regularly.

Goals should be SMART, meaning they are clear, quantifiable, achievable, relevant, and have deadlines. Get your goals out in the open, divide them into manageable chunks, and give yourself a deadline for each milestone. Incorporate your beliefs, interests, and aspirations into your goal-setting process. You may build a framework to direct your actions and maintain focus on what really matters by defining SMART goals.

You should also make it a point to evaluate your progress and make adjustments as necessary by setting goals. Journaling or other forms of self-reflection can help you make sense of your path by allowing you to reflect on your successes, failures, and lessons learned.

Take stock of your accomplishments, identify where you can grow, and reflect on anything that may have gotten in the way. Recognize and appreciate your achievements, and view failures as chances to learn and improve. One can develop self-awareness, resilience, and a growth mindset by prioritizing time for contemplation.

Teens can achieve their dreams with the help of sensible goal-setting. Teens can set themselves up for future success and fulfillment by prioritizing academic achievement, self-improvement, health, money, social impact, career exploration, digital responsibility, time management, cultural awareness, and goal planning. Remember that if you make explicit, quantifiable, achievable, and relevant goals and have a deadline, you can achieve them.

CONCLUSION

In concluding "Empowered Youth: Mastering Emotions and Stress - A CBT and DBT Guide for Teens," we emphasize the transformative power of understanding and managing one's mental well-being.

This guide has taken readers through an exploration of adolescent mental health, equipped them with essential CBT and DBT skills, and provided practical exercises for personal growth.

As adolescents navigate the challenges of today's world, the significance of effective coping strategies cannot be overstated. From recognizing and regulating emotions to embracing a growth mindset, the guide encourages teens to take charge of their mental health.

By integrating the principles of Cognitive Behavioral Therapy and Dialectical Behavior Therapy, this guide offers a holistic approach to building resilience.

The journey towards a resilient future involves setting goals, embracing personal growth, and fostering a positive mindset. We invite teens, parents, and educators to utilize the tools presented in this guide, creating a personalized mental wellness routine that empowers youth for lifelong success. In doing so, we contribute to a future where the mental health of our youth is prioritized, understood, and strengthened.

Bibliography

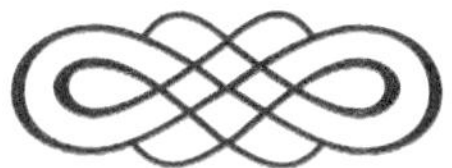

Beer-Becker, D. (2021, April 7). Creating Healthy Thinking Patterns: Your Brain Does Not Come Up With Truth, and Thought and Thinking are Two Different Things. Retrieved from Blake Psychology: https://www.blakepsychology.com/2020/01/creating-healthy-thinking-patterns-your-brain-does-not-come-up-with-truth-and-thought-and-thinking-are-two-different-things/

Compitus, D. K. (2020, Oct 1). What Are Distress Tolerance Skills? Your Ultimate DBT Toolkit. Retrieved from positivepsychology: https://positivepsychology.com/distress-tolerance-skills/

DBT Skills For Teens: This One DBT Skill Can Lift Most Teens' Negative Moods. (2020, Feb 4). Retrieved from EvolveTreatment: https://evolvetreatment.com/blog/dbt-skill-teens-moods/#:~:text=This%20is%20a%20good%20time,remain%20unobtrusive%2C%20and%20stay%20silent.

health, T. m. (2021, march 9). Understanding Emotions. Retrieved from Teenage mental health:

https://www.teenagementalhealth.co.uk/blog/post/13395/understanding-emotions/

HealthDirect. (2021, Oct). Teenage mental health. Retrieved from HealthDirect: https://www.healthdirect.gov.au/teenage-mental-health#:~:text=Do%20you%20ever%20feel%20alone,escapes%20through%20drugs%20and%20alcohol.

kidshealth. (n.d.). Understanding Your Emotions. Retrieved from Teens Health: https://kidshealth.org/en/teens/understand-emotions.html

McCarthy, C. (2022, March 8). The mental health crisis among children and teens: How parents can help. Retrieved from Health.Harvard: https://www.health.harvard.edu/blog/the-mental-health-crisis-among-children-and-teens-how-parents-can-help-202203082700

Miller, G. (2021, May 13). Dealing with Teen Emotions. Retrieved from psychcentral: https://psychcentral.com/blog/techniques-for-teens-how-to-cope-with-your-emotions

NewPortAcademy. (2020, Oct 30). A Guide to Teen Mental Disorders. Retrieved from NewPortAcademy: https://www.newportacademy.com/resources/mental-health/teen-mental-disorders/

Pietrangelo, A. (2019, Dec 12). 9 CBT Techniques for Better Mental Health. Retrieved from HealthLine: https://www.healthline.com/health/cbt-techniques#:~:text=In%20your%20first%20session%2C%20you,Specific

Sidney Deupree, M. L. (2023, August 11). CBT for Kids & Teens: How It Works, Examples, & Effectiveness. Retrieved from

Choosing Therapy: https://www.choosingtherapy.com/cbt-kids-teens/

sunrisertc. (2017, Sep 13). DBT Distress Tolerance Skills: Your 6-Skill Guide to Navigate Emotional Crises. Retrieved from sunrisertc: https://sunrisertc.com/distress-tolerance-skills/

Table of Contents. (n.d.). Retrieved from ClearforkAcademy: https://clearforkacademy.com/blog/dialectical-behavioral-therapy-for-teens-a-complete-guide/#:~:text=facing%20various%20issues.-,Introduction%20to%20Dialectical%20Behavioral%20Therapy%20(DBT),peer%20pressure%2C%20and%20increasing%20independence.

TurnBridge. (n.d.). 5 COMMON MENTAL HEALTH DISORDERS AMONG TEENS. Retrieved from TurnBridge: https://www.turnbridge.com/news-events/latest-articles/common-mental-health-disorders/#:~:text=Attention%20Deficit%20Hyperactivity%20Disorder%20(ADHD,to%20be%20facing%20ADHD%20today.

WHY IS THERE A RISE IN TEENAGE MENTAL HEALTH PROBLEMS? AN OVERVIEW OF STATISTICS. (n.d.). Retrieved from TurnBridge: https://www.turnbridge.com/news-events/latest-articles/rise-in-teenage-mental-health-problems/

9 798224 095742